Intel386™ Family Binary Compatibility Specification 2

Intel386™ Family Binary Compatibility Specification 2

Intel Corporation

McGraw-Hill, Inc.

New York St. Louis San Francisco Auckland Bogotá
Caracas Lisbon London Madrid Mexico Milan
Montreal New Delhi Paris San Juan São Paulo
Singapore Sydney Tokyo Toronto

Library of Congress Cataloging-in-Publication Data

Intel386 family binary compatibility specification 2 / Intel
    Corporation.
        p.   cm.—(Intel/McGraw-Hill series)
        Includes index.
        ISBN 0-07-031219-2 :
        1. Intel 80386 (Microprocessor)   I. Intel Corporation.
    II. Series.
    QA76.8.I2684I58   1991
    004.165—dc20   91-35732
                                              CIP

TRADEMARKS

2 3 4 5 6 7 8 9 0   DOH/DOH   9 7 6 5 4 3 2

ISBN   0-07-031219-2

Printed and bound by R. R. Donnelley & Sons Company.

Contents

1 INTRODUCTION

Intel386™ Family Binary Compatibility Specification   1-1
Foundations and Structure of the iBCS   1-2
How to Use the iBCS   1-3
Definition of Terms   1-6
Related Documents   1-7

2 SOFTWARE INSTALLATION

Introduction   2-1
Software Installation Media   2-2
OA&M Software Packaging   2-3
Installpkg Software Packaging   2-19
Custom Software Packaging   2-26

3 LOW-LEVEL SYSTEM INFORMATION

Introduction   3-1
Character Representations   3-2
Machine Interface   3-3
Function Calling Sequence   3-14
Operating System Interface   3-27
Coding Examples   3-50

4 OBJECT FILES

Introduction   4-1
COFF File Format   4-2
x.out File Format   4-12

5 PROGRAM LOADING

Program Loading   5-1

6 LIBRARIES

Introduction   6-1
C and System Services Library   6-3
Network Services Library   6-7
X-Windows Version 11 Release 4 Library   6-10
System Data Interfaces   6-28

7 SYSTEM FILE FORMATS

Introduction   7-1
Archive File   7-2
Other Archive Formats   7-7
Group File   7-8
Terminfo Data Base   7-9
Utmp File   7-12

8 SYSTEM COMMANDS

Commands for Application Programs   8-1

9 EXECUTION ENVIRONMENT

Application Environment   9-1
File System Structure and Contents   9-3
Console Device Control   9-8

Figures and Tables

Figure 2-1: Package File Tree Organization 2-4
Figure 2-2: Data Stream File Layout for Distribution Media 2-6
Figure 2-3: `installpkg` Media Format 2-19
Figure 2-4: Package File Tree Organization 2-20
Figure 2-5: `tar` Archive Format 2-26
Figure 2-6: Distribution Files Tree Organization 2-29
Figure 2-7: Example Permissions List 2-31
Figure 2-8: Example Product Name Usage 2-33
Figure 3-1: Scalar Types 3-4
Figure 3-2: Structure Smaller Than a Word 3-6
Figure 3-3: No Padding 3-6
Figure 3-4: Internal Padding 3-7
Figure 3-5: Internal and Tail Padding 3-7
Figure 3-6: `union` Allocation 3-8
Figure 3-7: Bit-Field Ranges 3-8
Figure 3-8: Bit Numbering 3-9
Figure 3-9: Right-to-Left Allocation 3-9
Figure 3-10: Boundary Alignment 3-10
Figure 3-11: Storage Unit Sharing 3-10
Figure 3-12: `union` Allocation 3-10
Figure 3-13: Unnamed Bit-Fields 3-11
Figure 3-14: Setting Memory Semaphore 3-12
Figure 3-15: Clearing Memory Semaphore 3-13
Figure 3-16: Test-and-Set Spinlock 3-13
Figure 3-17: Processor Registers 3-14
Figure 3-18: Standard Stack Frame 3-15
Figure 3-19: Function Prologue 3-20
Figure 3-20: Function Epilogue 3-20
Figure 3-21: Stack Contents for Functions Returning `struct/union` 3-22
Figure 3-22: Function Prologue (Returning `struct/union`) 3-23
Figure 3-23: Function Epilogue 3-23
Figure 3-24: Integral and Pointer Arguments 3-24
Figure 3-25: Floating-Point Arguments 3-25
Figure 3-26: Structure and Union Arguments 3-26
Figure 3-27: Virtual Address Configuration 3-27

Figure 3-28: System Call Template   3-30
Figure 3-29: System Call Numbers (in decimal)   3-31
Figure 3-30: Hardware Exceptions and Signals   3-37
Figure 3-31: Example `signal` Library Routine   3-40
Figure 3-32: Returning from Signal Handler   3-41
Figure 3-33: Signal State Structure   3-41
Figure 3-34: Intel387 Coprocessor State Structure   3-43
Figure 3-35: Declaration for `main`   3-44
Figure 3-36: EFLAGS Register Fields   3-45
Figure 3-37: Floating-Point Control Word   3-46
Figure 3-38: Initial Process Stack   3-46
Figure 3-39: Example Process Stack   3-49
Figure 3-40: Global Data Access Example   3-50
Figure 3-41: Local Data Access Example   3-51
Figure 3-42: Function Call Example   3-52
Figure 3-43: Indirect Function Call Example   3-53
Figure 3-44: Parameter Passing Example   3-53
Figure 3-45: Branch Instruction   3-55
Figure 3-46: `switch` Code   3-55
Figure 3-47: C Stack Frame   3-56
Figure 3-48: Argument Passing with `<varargs.h>`   3-58
Figure 3-49: Dynamic Stack Allocation   3-60
Figure 3-50: Processor Identification   3-62
Figure 4-1: COFF Object File Format   4-2
Figure 4-2: File Header   4-3
Figure 4-3: File Header Flags, `f_flags`   4-4
Figure 4-4: System Header   4-5
Figure 4-5: Magic Numbers in System Header   4-6
Figure 4-6: Section Header   4-7
Figure 4-7: Section Types, `s_flags`   4-8
Figure 4-8: Shared Library Section Entry   4-10
Figure 4-9: Example Shared Library Section   4-11
Figure 4-10: x.out Object File Format   4-12
Figure 4-11: x.out Header   4-13
Figure 4-12: Header Flags, `x_renv`   4-14
Figure 4-13: System Header   4-17
Figure 4-14: Segment Table   4-19
Figure 4-15: Segment Types, `xs_type`   4-21
Figure 4-16: Segment Attributes, `xs_attr`   4-22
Figure 4-17: Iteration Record   4-24

Figure 5-1: Segment Permissions   5-1
Figure 5-2: Executable File Example   5-2
Figure 5-3: Section Header Segments Example   5-3
Figure 5-4: Process Image Segments Example   5-4
Figure 6-1: System Library Names   6-2
Figure 6-2: libc Contents   6-3
Figure 6-3: libnsl Contents   6-7
Figure 6-4: libX11 Contents   6-10
Figure 6-5: <ctype.h>   6-30
Figure 6-6: <dirent.h>   6-31
Figure 6-7: <errno.h>, Part 1 of 3   6-32
Figure 6-8: <errno.h>, Part 2 of 3   6-33
Figure 6-9: <errno.h>, Part 3 of 3   6-34
Figure 6-10: <fcntl.h>, Part 1 of 2   6-35
Figure 6-11: <fcntl.h>, Part 2 of 2   6-36
Figure 6-12: <sys/fp.h>   6-36
Figure 6-13: <ftw.h>   6-37
Figure 6-14: <grp.h>   6-37
Figure 6-15: <ieeefp.h>   6-38
Figure 6-16: <sys/ipc.h>   6-39
Figure 6-17: <limits.h>, Part 1 of 2   6-40
Figure 6-18: <limits.h>, Part 2 of 2   6-41
Figure 6-19: <sys/lock.h>   6-41
Figure 6-20: <math.h>   6-42
Figure 6-21: <sys/mount.h>   6-42
Figure 6-22: <sys/msg.h>   6-43
Figure 6-23: <sys/param.h>   6-44
Figure 6-24: <poll.h>   6-45
Figure 6-25: <pwd.h>   6-45
Figure 6-26: <sys/reg.h>   6-46
Figure 6-27: <search.h>   6-46
Figure 6-28: <sys/sem.h>   6-47
Figure 6-29: <setjmp.h>   6-48
Figure 6-30: <sys/shm.h>   6-48
Figure 6-31: <signal.h>, Part 1 of 2   6-49
Figure 6-32: <signal.h>, Part 2 of 2   6-50
Figure 6-33: <sys/stat.h>, Part 1 of 2   6-51
Figure 6-34: <sys/stat.h>, Part 2 of 2   6-52
Figure 6-35: <sys/statfs.h>   6-53
Figure 6-36: <stddef.h>   6-53

Figure 6-37:	<stdio.h>, Part 1 of 2	6-54
Figure 6-38:	<stdio.h>, Part 2 of 2	6-55
Figure 6-39:	<stropts.h>, Part 1 of 3	6-56
Figure 6-40:	<stropts.h>, Part 2 of 3	6-57
Figure 6-41:	<stropts.h>, Part 3 of 3	6-58
Figure 6-42:	<sys/sysi86.h>	6-59
Figure 6-43:	<termios.h>, Part 1 of 11	6-60
Figure 6-44:	<termios.h>, Part 2 of 11	6-61
Figure 6-45:	<termios.h>, Part 3 of 11	6-62
Figure 6-46:	<termios.h>, Part 4 of 11	6-63
Figure 6-47:	<termios.h>, Part 5 of 11	6-64
Figure 6-48:	<termios.h>, Part 6 of 11	6-65
Figure 6-49:	<termios.h>, Part 7 of 11	6-66
Figure 6-50:	<termios.h>, Part 8 of 11	6-67
Figure 6-51:	<termios.h>, Part 9 of 11	6-68
Figure 6-52:	<termios.h>, Part 10 of 11	6-69
Figure 6-53:	<termios.h>, Part 11 of 11	6-70
Figure 6-54:	<sys/time.h>	6-71
Figure 6-55:	<sys/times.h>	6-72
Figure 6-56:	<sys/tiuser.h>, Error Return Values	6-73
Figure 6-57:	<sys/tiuser.h>, Event Bitmasks	6-74
Figure 6-58:	<sys/tiuser.h>, Flags	6-74
Figure 6-59:	<sys/tiuser.h>, Service Types	6-75
Figure 6-60:	<sys/tiuser.h>, Transport Interface Data Structures, 1 of 2	6-76
Figure 6-61:	<sys/tiuser.h>, Transport Interface Data Structures, 2 of 2	6-77
Figure 6-62:	<sys/tiuser.h>, Structure Types	6-78
Figure 6-63:	<sys/tiuser.h>, Fields of Structures	6-78
Figure 6-64:	<sys/tiuser.h>, Transport Interface States	6-79
Figure 6-65:	<sys/tiuser.h>, User-level Events	6-80
Figure 6-66:	<sys/types.h>	6-81
Figure 6-67:	<unistd.h>, Part 1 of 2	6-82
Figure 6-68:	<unistd.h>, Part 2 of 2	6-83
Figure 6-69:	<sys/utsname.h>	6-83
Figure 6-70:	<wait.h>	6-84
Figure 7-1:	<ar.h>	7-2
Figure 7-2:	Example String Table	7-4
Figure 7-3:	Archive Word Encoding	7-5
Figure 7-4:	Example Symbol Table	7-5
Figure 7-5:	Example Dump of a Compiled Description	7-11
Figure 7-6:	Utmp File Format	7-13

Figure 9-1: Floppy Disk Device Names — 9-6
Figure 9-2: Cartridge Tape Device Names — 9-7
Figure 9-3: Console Escape Sequences — 9-9
Figure 9-4: ioctl Type Definitions — 9-11
Figure 9-5: Console Keyboard Ioctls — 9-11
Figure 9-6: Level 2 Console Keyboard Ioctls — 9-12
Figure 9-7: Console Display Adapter/Virtual Terminal Ioctls — 9-13
Figure 9-8: Level 2 Console Display Adapter/Virtual Terminal Ioctls — 9-15
Figure 9-9: Reserved Ioctl Values — 9-17

Intel386™ Family Binary Compatibility Specification 2

1 INTRODUCTION

Intel386™ Family Binary Compatibility
Specification   1-1

Foundations and Structure of the iBCS   1-2

How to Use the iBCS   1-3
Base and Optional Components of the iBCS   1-4
Evolution of the iBCS   1-5

Definition of Terms   1-6

Related Documents   1-7

Intel386™ Family Binary Compatibility Specification

The **Intel386™ Family Binary Compatibility Specification**, or **iBCS**, defines a system interface for compiled application programs. Its purpose is to establish a standard binary interface for application programs on systems that implement the interfaces defined in the **System V Interface Definition, Issue 2**. This includes systems that have implemented various versions of the UNIX® operating system.

The iBCS defines a binary interface for application programs that are compiled and packaged for different UNIX implementations on many different hardware architectures using the Intel386 processor architecture family. The Intel386 processor architecture family includes the Intel386 processors, Intel486™ processors, and future compatible processors.

This document contains information specific to UNIX implementations built on the Intel386 processor architectures. It constitutes a complete **Intel386 Family Binary Compatibility Specification** for systems that implement the architecture of the Intel386 processors.

Foundations and Structure of the iBCS

The iBCS is based on several reference documents. Because it is a binary interface, it includes the fundamental set of machine instructions for the Intel386 processor to which the specification applies, and includes many other low-level specifications that may be strongly affected by the characteristics of the Intel386 processor's architecture. It also includes higher-level information based on the **System V Interface Definition, Issue 2**.

The interfaces specified here were drawn from existing standards for operating systems, user interfaces, programming languages, and networking, including those in the following list:

- The architecture manual for the Intel386 processor, especially the **Intel 80386 Programmer's Reference Manual**. All the information referenced by this supplement should be considered part of this specification, and just as binding as the requirements and data explicitly included here.

- The **System V Interface Definition**, or **SVID**. Issue 2 of the SVID was used as the basis for this issue of the iBCS.

- The **Portable Operating Systems Interfaces** Part 1, or **POSIX** Part 1. The 1988 version of the specification, published as IEEE P1003.1, is used as the basis for this issue of the iBCS. Only the interfaces specified in the 1988 version of POSIX.1 but not in the SVID Issue 2 are of interest for iBCS.

- The **X Window System Version 11, Release 4** or X11R4 interface specification.

The iBCS is divided into sections dealing with specific portions of the interface. Some sections contain detailed information, while others contain lists of interface components and pointers to other documents.

In general, this specification does not duplicate information that is available in other standards documents. For example, the iBCS section that describes system service routines includes a list of the system routines supported in this interface, formal declarations of the data structures they use that are visible to application programs, and a pointer to the **SVID** for information about the syntax and semantics of each call.

The iBCS identifies operating system components it includes, provides whatever information about those components that is not available elsewhere, and furnishes a reference to another document for further information. Information referenced in this way is as much a part of the iBCS specification as is the information explicitly included in this document.

How to Use the iBCS

The iBCS is a reference document that should be used in conjunction with the publicly-available standards documents it references. The iBCS enumerates the system components it includes, but descriptions of those components may be included entirely in the iBCS, partly in the iBCS and partly in other documents, or entirely in other reference documents.

Application developers who wish to produce binary packages that will install and run on any iBCS-based computer should follow this procedure:

1. Write programs that, when compiled and packaged, reference only the system calls, commands, and other facilities explicitly included in this specification. Note that kernel interfaces for device drivers are specifically excluded, because they may not be portable across different UNIX implementations.

2. Compile programs so that the resulting executable programs use the specified interfaces to system calls and have the format specified in the iBCS.

3. Package the application in the format and on the media described in this specification, and install or create files only in the specified locations provided for this purpose when the application is installed.

The manufacturers of iBCS-based computer systems who wish to provide the system interface described in this specification must satisfy a complementary set of requirements:

1. The system must implement the architecture described in the referenced hardware manual for the Intel386 processor.

2. The system must be capable of executing compiled programs having the format described in this specification.

3. The system's map of virtual memory must conform to the requirements of this specification.

4. The system's low-level behavior with respect to system call linkage, system traps, signals, and other such activities must conform to the formats documented in this specification.

5. The system must provide all commands, files, and utilities specified as part of the iBCS, in the format defined here and in other referenced documents. All commands and utilities must behave as documented in the **SVID**. The system must also provide all other components of an

application's environment that are included or referenced in the iBCS specification.

6. The system must install packages using the formats and procedures described in the iBCS, and must be capable of accepting installable software packages, either through physical media or through a network interface.

iBCS-conforming systems do not have to provide any compilation capabilities; even if a compilation system is provided, it need not generate iBCS-conforming executable files. However, the manufacturers of iBCS-based systems should identify some compilation system, not necessarily present on the iBCS-conforming system, that can compile source code into executable files that have the formats and characteristics specified in the iBCS.

Base and Optional Components of the iBCS

The iBCS provides two levels of interface specification: **Base** and **Optional**. **Base** components of the iBCS are required to be present in all conforming systems. **Optional** components may be absent on an iBCS-conforming system, but, when they are present, they must conform to the specification given in the iBCS. All components of the iBCS are to be considered **Base** components unless they are explicitly described as **Optional** components in the text of the specification. **Optional** components are marked with a note in the specification like the one that follows.

NOTE THE FACILITIES AND INTERFACES DESCRIBED IN THIS SECTION ARE OPTIONAL COMPONENTS OF the **Intel386 Family Binary Compatibility Specification**.

This distinction is necessary because some iBCS capabilities depend on the presence of hardware or other facilities that may not be present, such as integral graphics display or network connections and hardware. The absence of such facilities does not prevent a UNIX-based system from conforming with the iBCS specification, but it may prevent applications that need these facilities from running on those systems.

Evolution of the iBCS

The **Intel386 Family Binary Compatibility Specification** will evolve over time
to address new technology and market requirements, and will be reissued
approximately every three years. Each new edition of the specification is likely
to contain extensions and additions that will increase the potential capabilities of
applications that are written to conform to the iBCS.

As with the **System V Interface Definition**, the iBCS will implement **Level 1**
and **Level 2** support for its constituent parts. **Level 1** support indicates that a
portion of the specification will continue to be supported indefinitely, while
Level 2 support means that a portion of the specification may be withdrawn or
altered after the *next* edition of the iBCS is made available. That is, a portion of
the specification moved to **Level 2** support in an edition of the iBCS
specification will remain in effect at least until the following edition of the
specification is published.

All components of the iBCS have **Level 1** support unless they are explicitly
labeled as **Level 2**.

iBCS-conforming application programs should primarily or exclusively use
Level 1 interfaces. Level 2 interfaces are provided mostly for historical compatibility only. iBCS-conforming systems must implement both the Level 1
and Level 2 interfaces.

All the interfaces not specified in this revision of the iBCS specification are
reserved, including (but not limited to) system call numbers, `signal` numbers,
`errno` values, ioctl values, shared library addresses, and others. The manufacturers of iBCS-based computer systems may extend their system interface
beyond that described in this specification; however, the manufacturer must
contact Intel before extending the system interface to avoid any conflicts with
future revisions of the iBCS.

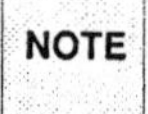

To request a reserved number, please write to:

iBCS Reserved Number Request
Intel Corporation
Mail Stop HF3-64
5200 Elam Young Parkway
Hillsboro, Oregon 97124

Definition of Terms

The following terms are used throughout this document.

- **iBCS**: Refers to the specification that is the subject of this document, the **Intel386 Family Binary Compatibility Specification**.

- **SVID**: Refers to the **System V Interface Definition** specification. Issue 2 of the SVID was used as the basis for this issue of the iBCS.

- **iBCS-conforming system**: A computer system that provides the binary system interface for application programs described in the iBCS.

- **iBCS-conforming program**: A program written to include only the system routines, commands, and other resources included in the iBCS, and a program compiled into an executable file that has the formats and characteristics specified for such files in the iBCS, and a program whose behavior complies with the rules given in the iBCS.

- **nonconforming program**: A program which has been written to include system routines, commands, or other resources not included in the iBCS, or a program which has been compiled into a format different from those specified in the iBCS, or a program which does not behave as specified in the iBCS.

- **undefined behavior**: Behavior that may vary from instance to instance or may change at some time in the future.

- **unspecified property**: A property of an entity that is not explicitly included or referenced in this specification, and may change at some time in the future. It is not good practice to make a program depend on an unspecified property.

Related Documents

The following documents may be of interest to the reader of this specification:

- *i486™ MICROPROCESSOR Programmer's Reference Manual* (Intel Literature order number 240486)

- *80386 Programmer's Reference Manual* (Intel Literature order number 230985)

- *80387 Programmer's Reference Manual* (Intel Literature order number 231917)

- *UNIX® System V/386 Programmer's Reference Manual*

- *UNIX® System V/386 Programmer's Guide*

- *UNIX® System V/386 System Administrator's Reference Manual*

- *System V Interface Definition*, Issue 2

- *Portable Operating System Interfaces (POSIX) -- Part 1*, IEEE P1003.1, 1988

- *Xlib - C Language X Interface, MIT X Consortium Standard, X Version 11, Release 4* by James Getty, Robert Scheifler and Ron Newman

2 SOFTWARE INSTALLATION

Introduction   2-1

Software Installation Media   2-2
Physical Distribution Media and Formats   2-2

OA&M Software Packaging   2-3
Media Format   2-3
Software Structure of the Physical Media   2-3
File Formats   2-8
- The pkginfo File   2-8
- The pkgmap File   2-10
- The copyright File   2-12
- The space File   2-13
- The depend File   2-13
- The compver File   2-14
- Installation and Removal Scripts   2-14
File Tree for Add-on Software   2-17
Commands that Install, Remove and Access Packages   2-17

Installpkg Software Packaging   2-19
Media Format   2-19
Software Structure of the Physical Media   2-20
File Formats   2-22
- The Size File   2-22
- The Name File   2-22
- The Install File   2-22
- The Remove File   2-23
- The Files File   2-24

■ Installation and Removal Scripts   2-24
File Tree for Add-on Software   2-24
Commands that Install, Remove and Access Packages   2-24

Custom Software Packaging   2-26
Media Format   2-26
Software Structure of the Physical Media   2-28
File Formats   2-30
    ■ The Label Directory   2-30
    ■ The Permissions List File   2-31
Configuration Scripts   2-36
    ■ Preparation Script   2-37
    ■ Initialization Script   2-37
    ■ Remove Script   2-37
File Tree for Add-on Software   2-38
Commands that Install, Remove and Access Packages   2-38

Introduction

This chapter defines how to package software that will be installed on an iBCS-conforming system. The physical and logical structures of a software package are described. Add-on software can be distributed using the supported physical media, and the software must be packaged with the specified logical file format or installation tools.

Software Installation Media

This section of the iBCS describes the media from which application software
can be installed on all iBCS-conforming systems. It includes the following
characteristics of supported media:

- Physical Distribution Media and Formats: Specification of the physical
  media that may be used to distribute iBCS-compliant application software.

- Media Format: Format of the software on the installation medium.

- Software Structure of the Physical Media: A functional description of the
  files contained on the physical media and their layout on the media.

Physical Distribution Media and Formats

Approved media for physical distribution of iBCS-conforming software are
listed below. Inclusion of a particular medium on this list does not require an
iBCS-conforming system to accept that medium. For example, a conforming
system may install all software through its network connection and accept none
of the listed media.

- 1.44MB 3 1/2" floppy disk: quad-density, double-sided, 80 tracks/side, 18
  sectors/track, 512 bytes/sector.

- 1.2MB 5 1/4" floppy disk: quad-density, double-sided, 80 tracks/side, 15
  sectors/track, 512 bytes/sector.

- 360KB 5 1/4" floppy disk: double-density, double-sided, 40 tracks/side, 9
  sectors/track, 512 bytes/sector.

- 60MB quarter-inch cartridge tape in QIC-24 format.

The QIC-24 cartridge tape data format is described in *Proposed Standard for Data
Interchange on the Streaming 1/4 Inch Magnetic Tape Cartridge Using Group Code
Recording at 10000 FRPI*, Revision D, April 22, 1983. This document is available
from the Quarter-Inch Committee (QIC) through Freeman Associates, 311 East
Carillo St., Santa Barbara, CA 93101.

OA&M Software Packaging

Media Format

Packages are stored as a continuous data stream on the distribution media. The continuous data stream is valid for all media. The data stream can be created using the dd(AU_CMD) and cpio(BU_CMD) utilities.

Software Structure of the Physical Media

Add-on application software is bundled and installed in units called packages. Multiple packages can be delivered on a single volume of media, or a package can span multiple volumes of media. A package that spans multiple volumes of media must be the only package on those volumes.

Software to be bundled as a package must be organized as a file tree subdirectory as shown in Figure 2-1. The data stream from the distribution media is read onto disk into a file subtree of this format before the actual installation begins. Figure 2-2 shows the sequence of files in the data stream stored on distribution media.

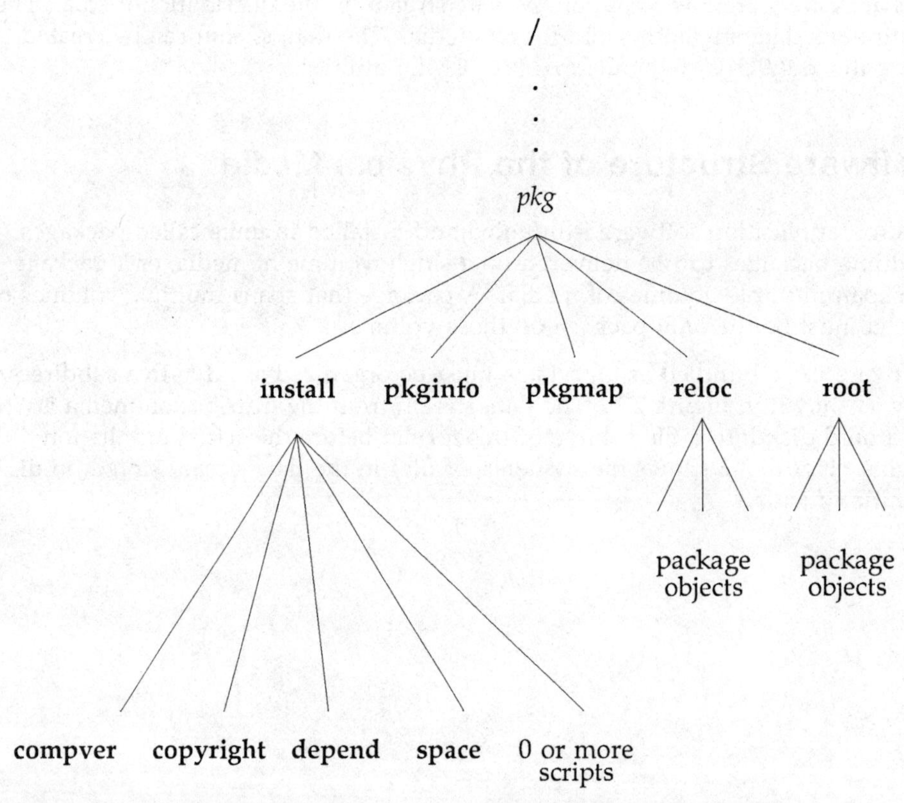
/
.
.
.
pkg
install
pkginfo
pkgmap
reloc
root
package
objects
package
objects
compver
copyright
depend
space
0 or more
scripts

The following is a brief description of the files and directories shown in Figure 2-1. Entries in **bold** type are standard file or directory names; the names of the other items are package-specific.

The following files are required:

- **pkginfo**: describes the package.

- **pkgmap**: describes each package object (files, directories, etc.).

The following files and directories are optional:

- **compver**: describes previous versions of the package with which this version is compatible.

- **copyright**: copyright notice for the package.

- **depend**: describes dependencies and incompatibilities across packages.

- **install**: contains optional package information files.

- package objects: executables, data files, etc., belonging to the package.

- **reloc**: contains relocatable package objects (files whose pathnames on the target system are determined at the time of installation rather than at the time of package creation).

- **root**: contains non-relocatable package objects.

- **space**: describes space requirements beyond package objects.

- scripts: zero or more scripts to handle package-specific installation and removal requirements.

Figure 2-2: Data Stream File Layout for Distribution Media

<table>
<tr><td>header:</td><td># PaCkAgE DaTaStReAm[: type]
pkgA num_parts max_part_size [N ... N]
pkgB num_parts max_part_size [N ... N]
.
.
.
end of header</td></tr>
<tr><td>special information
files (cpio archive):</td><td>pkgA/pkginfo
pkgA/pkgmap
pkgB/pkginfo
pkgB/pkgmap
.
.
.</td></tr>
<tr><td>package part
(cpio archive):</td><td>pkgA/pkginfo
pkgA/install/*
pkgA/root.1/*
pkgA/reloc.1/*</td></tr>
<tr><td>package part
(cpio archive):</td><td>pkgA/pkginfo
pkgA/root.2/*
pkgA/reloc.2/*</td></tr>
<tr><td></td><td>.
.
.</td></tr>
<tr><td>package part
(cpio archive):</td><td>pkgB/pkginfo
pkgB/install/*
pkgB/root.1/*
pkgB/reloc.1/*</td></tr>
<tr><td></td><td>.
.
.</td></tr>
</table>

The data stream format begins with a header containing ASCII characters. A special character string on the first line identifies the start of the header. It should be in the following format:

 # PaCkAgE DaTaStReAm[: type]

When no *type* is defined, the data stream is continuous. Additional types of data streams may be specified at a later date. Such additional types would deal with media-specific physical storage attributes, for example, record size, blocking factors, or alignment of package parts on the media.

Next are one or more special lines, one for each package in the distribution. Each line has the following format:

pkginstance   num_parts   max_part_size   [N ... N]

where:

- *pkginstance* is the package identifier made up of the package mnemonic (described later as the **PKG** parameter in the **pkginfo** file) and an optional suffix.

- *num_parts* is the number of parts into which the package is divided. As shown in Figure 2-2, a part is a collection of files contained in a cpio(BU_CMD) archive. A part is the atomic unit by which a package is processed. Each part must fit entirely on a distribution media volume, i.e., a part cannot cross volumes. A developer chooses the criteria for grouping files into a part.

- *max_part_size* is the maximum number of 512-byte blocks consumed by a single part of the package.

- *N ... N* are optional fields to indicate the number of parts stored on the sequential volumes of media which contain the package. For example,

pkgA 6 2048 2 3 1

indicates that *pkgA* consists of six parts. The largest part is 2048 512-byte blocks in size. The first two parts exist on the first volume, the next three parts exist on the second volume, and the last part exists on the third, and last, volume. These fields only apply where multiple volumes are needed to distribute a package. Otherwise, these fields should not appear and any process reading the header should assume that all parts of the package reside on the current volume. When these fields are used, there can only be one package in the data stream.

A special character string on a separate line identifies the end of the header. It should be in the following format:

 # end of header

The header must be padded to a 512-byte boundary.

Following the header is a cpio(BU_CMD) archive (with the –c option) containing special information files for each package. The rest of the data stream consists of package parts. Note that a given package may consist of one or more parts, i.e., cpio(BU_CMD) archives. A package which requires multiple parts must meet the following conditions:

- Each part must contain the entire **pkginfo** file.

- Each part must include its own **root** and **reloc** directories and these directories are numbered. For example, a package that requires n parts has **root.1** and **reloc.1** through **root.n** and **reloc.n**. n is limited to eight digits.

- The **install** directory and its contents must be provided in the first part only.

File Formats

The pkginfo File

The **pkginfo** file describes the package, as a whole. Each line is of the form *parameter=value*. The list below describes defined parameters. These parameters can be retrieved via pkginfo(AS_CMD) and/or have a specific meaning to the package installation and removal commands (pkgadd(AS_CMD) and pkgrm(AS_CMD)). No specific ordering of parameters is required. Lines beginning with '#' are treated as comments.

- PKG: Package mnemonic, limited to 9 characters. The first character must be alphabetic; remaining characters can be alphabetic, numeric, or the characters '+' and '–'. **install**, **new**, and **all** are not valid package mnemonics.

- **NAME**: Package name, limited to 256 ASCII characters.

- **ARCH**: A comma-separated list of identifiers that specify the architecture(s) on which the package can run. Each architecture identifier is limited to 16 ASCII characters; the character ' **,** ' is invalid.

- **VERSION**: Version identifier, limited to 256 ASCII characters. The first character cannot be a left parenthesis due to the syntax of the **depend** file. This identifier is vendor-specific information.

- **DESC**: Descriptive text, limited to 256 ASCII characters.

- **VENDOR**: Vendor identifier, limited to 256 ASCII characters.

- **HOTLINE**: Phone number or mailing address where further information may be requested or bugs reported. The value of this parameter is limited to 256 ASCII characters.

- **EMAIL**: An electronic mail address, with the same purpose and length limitation as the **HOTLINE** parameter.

- **VSTOCK**: Vendor stock number, limited to 256 ASCII characters.

- **CATEGORY**: A comma-separated list of categories to which the package belongs. Add-on software packages must state their membership in the **application** category. Users can request information on all packages in specific categories via pkginfo(AS_CMD). Category identifiers are case-insensitive and are limited to 16 alphanumeric characters, excluding the space and comma characters.

- **PSTAMP**: Production stamp, limited to 256 ASCII characters. This is used to distinguish between different production versions.

- **ISTATES**: Space-separated list of valid run-levels during which this package can be installed. Run-levels are integers in the range 0 through 6, **s** and **S** (see **SVID**, init(AS_CMD)).

- **RSTATES**: Same as **ISTATES**, but applies to package removal.

- **ULIMIT**: Temporary file size limit to use during installation of this package (see **SVID**, getrlimit(BA_OS)).

- **INTONLY**: A parameter that indicates a package can only be installed interactively by the pkgadd(AS_CMD) command. If this parameter is supplied and set to any non-null value (e.g., '**y**' or "yes"), the package can only be installed interactively. Otherwise, the package can be installed in a noninteractive mode using pkgask(AS_CMD) or pkgadd with the −n option.

- **MAXINST**: An integer that specifies the maximum number of instances of this package that can be installed on a system at one time. If this parameter is not supplied, a default of 1 is used (that is, at most one copy of the package can be installed on a system at any time).

- **BASEDIR**: A default value (which can be overridden at the time of installation) for the directory in which relocatable files will be installed. Pathnames of package objects that start with a character other than '/' or '$' have the value of this parameter and the character '/' prepended in order to determine the location in which they will be installed; it must be a legal directory name.

- **CLASSES**: A space-separated list of package object classes to be installed. Every package object is assigned to one class (in the **pkgmap** file). Class assignment can be used to control which objects are installed (for example, based on administrator input at the time of installation), and to provide specific actions to be taken to install or remove them. The value of this parameter can be overridden at the time of installation.

PKG, NAME, ARCH, VERSION and **CATEGORY** are mandatory parameters, i.e., package developers must supply them. The rest are optional.

Other parameters may be defined in the **pkginfo** file. If they are used as part of package object pathnames in the **pkgmap** file, the value supplied in the **pkginfo** file is used as a default and may be overridden at the time of installation. Other parameters will be made part of the environment in which installation scripts execute.

The pkgmap File

Each line in the **pkgmap** file describes a package object or installation script (with the exception of one **pkgmap** entry, described at the end of this section). The following list describes the space-separated fields in each **pkgmap** entry; their order must be the same as in the list. Lines in the file that begin with '#' are ignored.

part A positive integer that indicates the part of a multi-part package in which this pathname resides.

ftype A one-character file type identifier from the set below:

f - a file.

d - a directory.

i - an installation or removal script.

l - a linked file.

p - a named pipe.

b - a block special device.

c - a character special device.

e - a file installed or removed by editing.

v - a volatile file, whose contents are expected to change as the package is used on the system.

x - an exclusive directory, which should contain only files installed as part of this or some other standard format package.

class A package object class identifier, limited to 12 characters. **none** is used to specify no class membership. This field is not specified for files whose *ftype* is **i**.

pathname The pathname describing the location of the file on the target machine. For files of *ftype* **l**, *pathname* must be of the form *path1=path2*, specifying the destination (*path1*) and source (*path2*) files to be linked.

The *pathname* may contain variables that support relocation of the file. A *$parameter* may be embedded in the pathname structure. **$BASEDIR** can be used to identify the parent directories of the path hierarchy, making the entire package easily relocatable. Default values for *parameter* and **BASEDIR** must be supplied in the **pkginfo** file and may be overridden at installation.

major
    The major device number, only appears for files whose *ftype* is **b** or **c**.

minor
    The minor device number, only appears for files whose *ftype* is **b** or **c**.

mode
    The octal mode of the file. ' ? ' indicates that no particular mode is required. This field is not provided for files whose *ftype* is l or i.

owner
    The *uid* of the owner of the file; it must be a legal *uid*. ' ? ' indicates that no particular owner is required. This field is not provided for files whose *ftype* is l or i.

group
    The group to which the file belongs, limited to 14 characters. ' ? ' indicates that no particular group is required. This field is not provided for files whose *ftype* is l or i.

size
    The file size in bytes. This field is not provided for files whose *ftype* is **d, x, p, b, c,** or **l**.

cksum
    The checksum of the file contents, as calculated by **sum**(1). This field is not provided for files whose *ftype* is **d, x, p, b, c,** or **l**.

modtime
    The time of last modification as reported by **stat**(BA_OS). The time is given as the number of seconds that have elapsed since 00:00 Jan. 1, 1970 (GMT). This field is not provided for files whose *ftype* is **d, x, p, b, c** or **l**.

An additional line in the **pkgmap** file, beginning with a colon, provides information about the media on which the package is distributed. Its format is:

    : *number_of_parts maximum_part_size*

number_of_parts specifies the number of parts which compose this package. *maximum_part_size* specifies the size, in 512-byte blocks, of the largest part.

The copyright File

The contents of the **copyright** file will be displayed on *stdout* at the time of installation; there are no format requirements.

The space File

The **space** file describes disk block and inode requirements for the package beyond files listed in the **pkgmap** file and provided on the media. Each line in the file contains the following three space-separated fields:

pathname   A directory name. Naming conventions (with respect to indicating relocatability) are the same as for the *pathname* field in the **pkgmap** file.

blocks   The number of 512-byte blocks required.

inodes   The number of distinct files required.

The depend File

The **depend** file describes dependencies across packages. The format of each entry is as follows, with space-separated fields:

> *type pkg name*
> *(arch)version*

The following field definitions and rules apply:

type   Describes the type of dependency:

> **P -**   a prerequisite for installation.
>
> **I -**   an incompatibility.
>
> **R -**   reverse dependency (the referenced package depends on this package).

pkg   The package mnemonic, as defined in the **pkginfo** file.

name   The package name, as defined in the **pkginfo** file.

arch   The package architecture, as defined in the **pkginfo** file.

version   The package version, as defined in the **pkginfo** file.

There may be zero or more *(arch)version* lines, *(arch)version* lines must begin with white space.

The compver File

The **compver** file specifies previous versions of the package with which this version is compatible. It is used for dependency checking across packages, in conjunction with the **depend** file. It consists of version identifiers, as defined in the **pkginfo** file, one per line.

Installation and Removal Scripts

This section describes installation and removal scripts that may be provided by a package to meet package-specific needs. Scripts are executed by sh(BU_CMD) and therefore must be either shell scripts or executable programs. In the case of recovery from an interrupted installation they may be re-executed; they should be written so that multiple invocations produce the same results as a single invocation.

The request Script

The **request** script, if provided, is the first script executed at the time of package installation. Its purpose is to interact with the user and modify details of the installation process as a result of this interaction. The script writes shell variable assignments to the file named by its only argument. It is executed with *uid* **install** and *gid* **other**. **stdin**, **stdout** and **stderr** are all attached to /**dev/tty**. The **CLASSES** variable is defined as part of the installation procedure and may be set by the **request** script.

Procedure Scripts

Four scripts may be provided by a package to handle package-specific requirements - **preinstall**, **postinstall**, **preremove** and **postremove**. The following constraints apply to these procedure scripts:

- When the script is executed, **stdin** is attached to /**dev/null**; **stdout** and **stderr** are attached to /**dev/tty**.

- Each pathname created or modified by a procedure script during installation or removal, and which should be considered part of the package, must be logically added or removed from the package via the installf(AS_CMD) or removef(AS_CMD) commands.

- Procedure scripts are executed with *uid* **root** and *gid* **other**.

The **preinstall** and **postinstall** scripts are executed before and after the installation of the package by the installation class scripts, respectively. The **preremove** and **postremove** scripts are execute before and after the removal of the package by the removal class scripts, respectively.

Class Scripts

Class scripts provide alternate installation and removal actions for classes of package objects (the membership of objects in a class is specified in the **pkgmap** file). The following constraints apply:

- Each class of objects included in the value of the **CLASSES** parameter is installed, in the order in which it appears in that parameter. Objects in class **none** are installed first.

- If an object belongs to class **none** or no class script is provided for the class, the object is copied from the medium to the target system during installation, and removed during removal.

- Class script names are of the form *operation.class*, where *operation* is either **i** (for install) or **r** (for remove), and *class* is the class name, limited to 12 characters. Class names beginning with 'O' (hex 0x4f) are reserved.

- Class scripts will execute as *uid* **root** and *gid* **other**.

- During installation, the class script is executed with either no arguments or the single argument **ENDOFCLASS**. **stdin** contains a list of filename pairs, of the form *source_pathname destination_pathname*. The *source_pathname* parameter is either a pathname on the medium or **/dev/null** to indicate there is no file to copy from the medium (for example, a directory). *destination_pathname* is the target pathname. Only files that are members of the class and are not identical to files already on the system are provided to the script.

- The class script is invoked with the single argument **ENDOFCLASS** to indicate that there are no more files belonging to the class once end of file is reached on **stdin** during the current invocation of the script.

- During removal, the class script is executed with no arguments. **stdin** contains a list of filenames, including all members of the class except those shared by other installed packages whose *ftype* in the **pkgmap** file is something other than **e**.

■ Three standard classes are defined — **build, sed** and **awk**. The name of the file on the medium is the name of the file on the target system to be modified.

For the **sed** and **awk** classes, the file provided on the medium contains sed(BU_CMD) or awk(BU_CMD) instructions. Lines of the format **!install** and **!remove** mark the beginning of instructions that apply to installation and removal, respectively. The file on the target system will be modified by the output of **sed** or **awk**, using the provided data.

A file that belongs to the **build** class is executed with a single argument, **install** or **remove**. Its output (on **stdout**) is written to the file it references on the target system.

Exit Codes used by Scripts

Scripts can exit with an additive combination of one of the first four and one of the last two exit codes listed below:

0:	successful execution.
1:	fatal error.
2:	warning.
3:	interruption.
10:	reboot after installation of all packages.
20:	reboot after installation of this package.

For example, the exit code for a script resulting in a warning condition and that requires an immediate reboot is **22**.

File Tree for Add-on Software

/opt, /var/opt and /etc/opt are reserved in the file tree for the installation of application software packages. Each add-on software package should adhere to the following rules:

- Static package objects should be installed in /opt/*pkg*, where *pkg* is the package mnemonic or instance.

- Package objects that change in normal operations (for example, log and spool files) should be installed in /var/opt/*pkg*.

- Machine-specific configuration files should be installed in /etc/opt/*pkg*.

- Executables that are directly invoked by users should be installed in /opt/*pkg*/**bin**.

- Only package objects that must reside in specific locations within the system file tree in order to function properly (for example, special files in /**dev**) should be installed in those locations.

Commands that Install, Remove and Access Packages

The following commands and library routines are used to install and remove packages and to retrieve information about installed packages. They will be included in every iBCS-conforming system, and are defined in the **SVID**.

`pkgadd`(AS_CMD):	installs packages.
`pkgrm`(AS_CMD):	removes packages.
`pkgchk`(AS_CMD):	checks installed packages.
`pkginfo`(AS_CMD):	display information about packages.
`pkgask`(AS_CMD):	runs the request script and stores output for later use.
`installf`(AS_CMD):	associates an installed file with a package.
`removef`(AS_CMD):	removes a file's association with a package.

pkgparam(AS_CMD):   display the values of parameters defined by the package in the **pkginfo** file.

Installpkg Software Packaging

The **installpkg** installation format described in this section is at Level 2.

Media Format

Packages are stored as a continuous data stream on the distribution media. The continuous data stream is valid for all media. The data stream can be created using the dd(AU_CMD) and cpio(BU_CMD) utilities as described in the **SVID**.

Multiple packages can be distributed only on cartridge tape media. If the media is to contain multiple packages, then the first file on the first volume must be the special file **pkglist**. The structure of the distribution media is shown in Figure 2-3:

Figure 2-3: `installpkg` **Media Format**

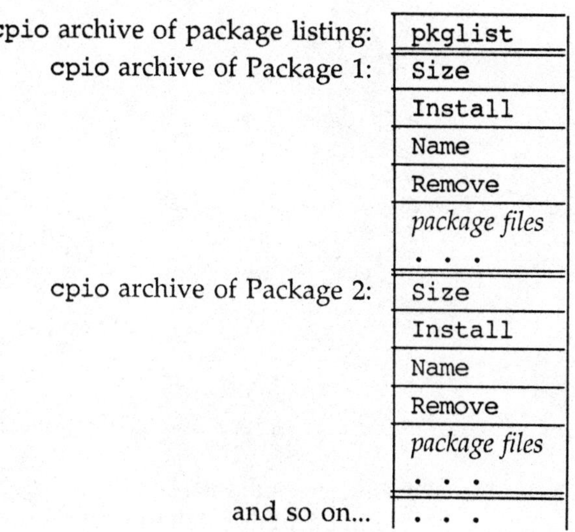

The **pkglist** file is a list of the names of the packages contained on the media.

Packages must be listed in the order that they appear on the media. This file is present only if multiple packages are stored on the media.

Software Structure of the Physical Media

Add-on application software is bundled and installed in units called packages. Multiple packages can be delivered on a single volume of media, or a package can span multiple volumes of media. A package that spans multiple volumes of media must be the only package on those volumes.

Software to be bundled as a package can be organized in any manner that is suitable for the application, except that the special files **Size**, **Name**, **Install**, **Remove**, and **Files** must be at the "**./**" level and none of the package files can have absolute pathnames. Figure 2-4 shows the collection of special files in the data stream stored on distribution media.

Figure 2-4: Package File Tree Organization

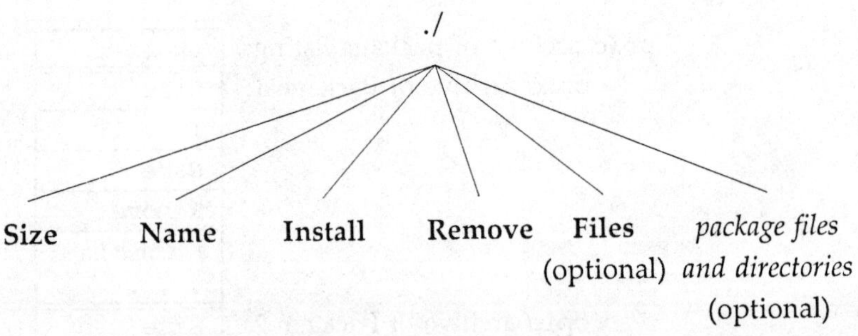

The data stream from the distribution media is read onto disk into a temporary file subtree of this format before the actual installation begins.

The following is a brief description of the special files shown in Figure 2-4. Entries in bold type are standard file or directory names; the names of the other items are package-specific.

The following files are required:

- **Size**: an ASCII file that contains information about the size of the package.

- **Name**: an ASCII file that describes the package being installed.

- **Install**: an executable file or shell script executed *after* the files are copied into a temporary area and *before* they are removed from the temporary installation directory.

- **Remove**: an executable file or shell script to remove the software package.

The following files and directories are optional:

- **Files**: contains the full pathnames of the files that are being installed. The file can either be from the installation media or created by the **Install** program.

- *package files and directories*: zero or more package-specific files or subdirectories.

The data stream format is a cpio(BU_CMD) archive, as specified in the **SVID**. The installation media should be created with the cpio command with the −c option specified. It is imperative that the −c option be used since the installation program that reads the media assumes this format.

The list of pathnames that drives the cpio command has two restrictions:

1. **All pathnames MUST be relative (NOT begin with a '/').** This is because the cpio command will copy the files into the temporary directory before the **Install** program moves them into their permanent locations.

2. The first entry of the list should be **Size**. If the application requires more than one volume, the **Size** file must be on the first volume and should appear first.

Following the **Size** special file should be the pathnames (without a leading '/') for all files to be placed on the media.

File Formats

The Size File

The **Size** file may be a single- or double-record file. It contains the number of blocks required on the root (/) and user (/**usr**) file systems to install and use the application package. A block is defined as 512 bytes.

Each number put in the **Size** file should be the larger of the two:

1. number of blocks that are used while installing the package; or

2. amount of blocks used up on the system once the package is installed and exercised by the user.

The lines in the **Size** file have the following formats:

> USR=<*number of blocks required on* /usr>
> ROOT=<*number of blocks required on* />

These lines can be in reverse order, with *no* spaces on either side of the equal sign.

The Name File

The **Name** file contains the name of the product as it is to appear during the installation and removal operations. This file is a single record (or single line) and can contain up to 65 characters of significant data (only the first 65 characters are displayed in the menus). The **Name** file is used to determine whether the package has been previously installed. It should be unique. Do not use shell metacharacters (for example, '/', '*', '?', '[', ']', '&', '!', '$'), or single or double quotes in the **Name** file.

The Install File

The **Install** file is an executable program or shell script.

Transferral of Program From the Temporary Directory

The **Install** program will not be invoked until all the programs and files on all volumes have been copied into the temporary directory. After that, the **Install** program will modify them as needed (for example, change mode or change ownership). The files will then be ready to be moved into their intended file system destination. The transfer (move) is usually a straightforward operation, but there are some common stumbling blocks.

- **Permissions**: The permissions should be acceptable when created by the cpio command. Executables should have the correct executable permissions set, and read-write permissions should be such that the normal user can use them as required. The **setuid** bit should also be set where appropriate.

- **Ownership**: In general, files should be owned by standard system users (for example, **root, bin, uucp, lp, install**, etc.). Be careful not to include files that are owned by local users with specific machine ownership (such as the machine where the files were created).

- **Temporary Files**: If any intermediate files are created, they must be placed in the temporary directory to ensure that fragments are not left. installpkg removes this temporary directory at the end of the installation.

Installation of Libraries, Include Files, Etc.

The installation program must not overwrite or modify any existing system files, executables, libraries, include files.

Communication with the User

All communication with the user should be by means of the standard input and output (**stdin/stdout**, or the read and echo commands if it is a shell script). It is generally advisable to keep the user informed as to the state of events, especially delays. When difficulties arise, alternative procedures can be presented and the user consulted. Ask the user for verification when necessary. The installpkg command issues its own completion message.

The Remove File

The **Remove** file is an executable program. It is invoked by the removepkg command to remove a previously installed package. The **Remove** program, once executed, should leave the system in the same state it would have been in had the new application never been installed. Depending on the situation, files created by the application may also need to be removed. This is, however, something for the user to decide, and it is recommended that users be consulted before attempting to remove any user-owned files.

The Files File

The **Files** file is an optional file. It contains the full pathnames of the files that are being installed. **Files** must list the absolute pathname for each file contained on the software installation media or created by the **Install** program. The names must be completely enumerated and contain no wildcard characters (for example, '*', '?', etc.). The pathnames are listed one per line.

Installation and Removal Scripts

This section describes installation and removal scripts that is provided by a package to meet package-specific needs. Scripts are executed by sh(BU_CMD) and therefore must be either shell scripts or executable programs. In the case of recovery from an interrupted installation they may be re-executed; they should be written so that multiple invocations produce the same results as a single invocation.

File Tree for Add-on Software

/usr/lib/installed and /usr/options are reserved in the file tree for the installation of application software packages. Each add-on software package should adhere to the following rules:

- installpkg will create a summary of the package installed based on the contents of the **Name** file, as well as copy any **Files** file and the **Remove** file to the /usr/lib/installed directory.

- installpkg will create a summary of the package installed in /usr/options, based on the contents of the **Name** file.

Commands that Install, Remove and Access Packages

The following commands and library routines are used to install and remove packages and to retrieve information about installed packages. They will be included in every iBCS-conforming system.

installpkg: installs packages.

removepkg: removes packages.

displaypkg: display information about packages.

Custom Software Packaging

Media Format

Packages are stored as a continuous data stream on the distribution media. The continuous data stream is valid for all media. The data stream can be created using the `tar`(AU_CMD) utility.

Each file archived by `tar` is in contiguous blocks, with the header in the first block and the file occupying the following blocks. Figure 2-5 shows the structure of the `tar` archive.

Figure 2-5: `tar` **Archive Format**

<table>
<tr><td align="right">File 1 Header:</td><td>Header Block</td></tr>
<tr><td></td><td>File Blocks</td></tr>
<tr><td></td><td>. . .</td></tr>
<tr><td></td><td>EOF</td></tr>
<tr><td align="right">File 2 Header:</td><td>Header Block</td></tr>
<tr><td></td><td>File Blocks</td></tr>
<tr><td></td><td>. . .</td></tr>
<tr><td></td><td>EOF</td></tr>
<tr><td align="right">and so on...</td><td>. . .</td></tr>
</table>

All headers and file data blocks start on 512-byte boundaries and are tail padded if necessary. Header blocks are padded with nulls and file data blocks are padded with undefined values. The format of the `tar` archive header block is as follows:

```
#define TBLOCK                  512
#define NBLOCK                  20
#define NAMSIZ                  100

union hblock {
        char dummy[TBLOCK];
        struct header {
                char name[NAMSIZ];
                char mode[8];
                char uid[8];
                char gid[8];
                char size[12];
                char mtime[12];
                char chksum[8];
                char linkflag;
                char linkname[NAMSIZ];
                char extno[4];
                char extotal[4];
                char efsize[12];
        } dbuf;
} dblock;
```

name is the pathname of the file when archived. If the pathname starts with a
null character, the file is empty and the rest of the header is not examined. Otherwise the pathname is null terminated. The *mode, uid, gid, size,* and *time* fields
are the octal character representations of the corresponding fields of the inode
structure for the file; these fields are null terminated.

extno must be set to zero (0). The *extotal* and *efsize* fields are ignored. *chksum*
field has a value such that the sum of all the bytes of the header block is zero.

If *linkflag* is set to 0 (zero), then there are no links and the *linkname* field is
ignored. If *linkflag* is set to 1 (one), then *linkname* contains the pathname of the
file to which this entry is linked.

The `custom` utility installs, lists, and removes software.   `custom` automatically
determines the media format from the following types:

Size	Device	Size in 512-Byte Blocks
5.25"	48ds9	720
5.25"	96ds9	1440
5.25"	96ds15	2400
3.5"	135ds9	1440
3.5"	135ds18	2880

Software Structure of the Physical Media

Add-on application software is grouped into and installed as units called packages. A package is a logical group of files; a package groups files into functional units that can be installed as desired — either all packages together or individually. Multiple packages can be delivered on a single volume of media, or a package can span multiple volumes of media. A single file cannot span between media volumes.

Figure 2-6: Distribution Files Tree Organization

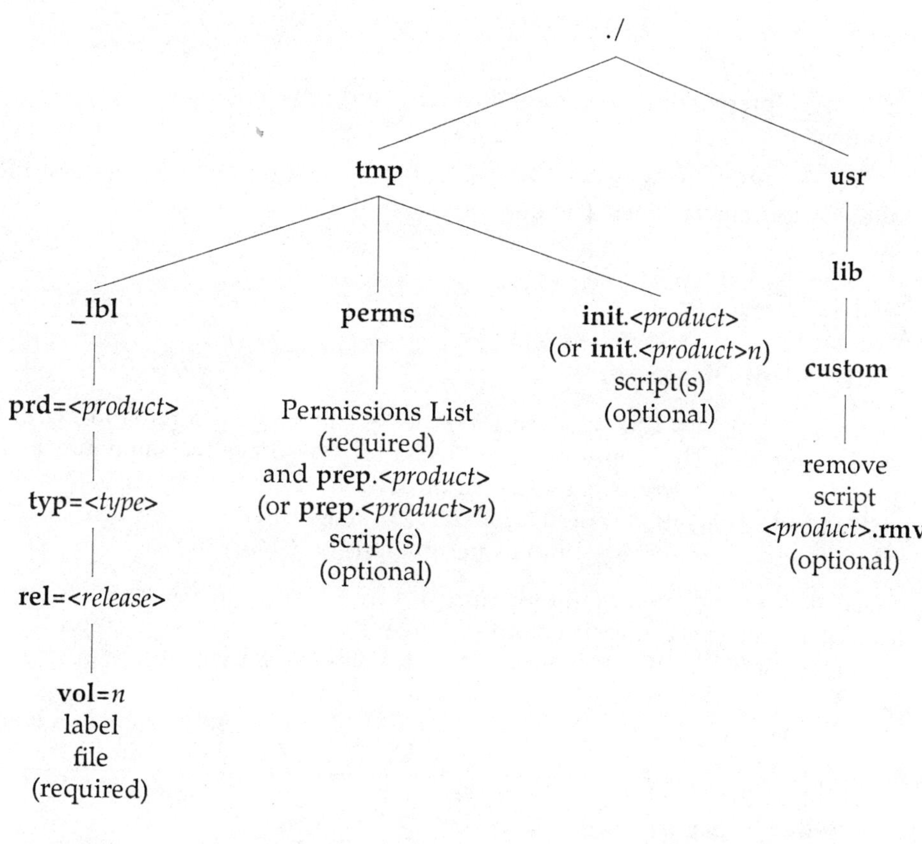

The following is a brief description of the files and directories shown in Figure 2-6. Entries in Figure 2-6 in bold type are standard file or directory names; the names of the other items are package- or product-specific.

The following directories and files are required:

- The label directory: **_lbl**.

- The permissions list: **perms**.

The **prep** (preparation), **init** (initialization), and **rmv** (remove) scripts are optional.

The distribution media format begins with the label directory as the first file on the distribution volume. The only other required file is the permissions list.

File Formats

The Label Directory

The label directory contains a series of nested directories culminating with a single empty file. The names of the nested directories have the same information as values in the permissions list. All directories are owned by *root/other* and have permissions modes of 0755. The zero-length file in the release directory has the same ownerships, but has permissions of 0444.

The label directory starts in the ./tmp/_lbl directory on the distribution media and is the first file on each volume of the distribution media. The format for the names of the subdirectories under the label directory are:

Directory or File	Permissions List Keyword	Name Length in Characters
./tmp/_lbl		
prd=*<product name>*	#prd	8
typ=*<CPU or system type>*	#typ	10
rel=*<Product release number>*	#rel	10
vol=*<Distribution media volume number>*	*none*	10

Refer to the next section for more information on the permissions list keywords. All values to the right of the equals sign are vendor-defined and can be a maximum of 8 or 10 characters in length as described above. The only restriction on the names is that the values in each directory name must agree with its respective permissions list keyword, and that the permissions list have the same filename as the **prd=** value, which is a mnemonic name of the product.

The Permissions List File

The permissions list file contains an entry for each file in the distribution. The permissions list is located on the distribution media in the ./**tmp/perms** directory. The name of the permissions list is a mnemonic name of the product and is 8 or less alphabetic characters. Only one permissions list is permitted per product. The name of the permissions list is the same value in the #prd keyword in the permissions list.

The permissions list file has the following format: if a line starts with a pound character ('#') and a space, it is a comment. If the line starts with a pound character and an exclamation sign ('!'), or a pound character and a letter from 'a' to 'z', then it is a special keyword phrase. Only the keywords described in the next section are currently defined. Non-blank lines not starting with a pound character are description lines. The custom utility parses the keyword phrases and description lines to determine what is being installed or, in the case of directories or device files, created. There is one item specification per line. Figure 2-7 shows an example permissions list file.

Figure 2-7: Example Permissions List

```
 1     # Small OS Permissions List
 2     #
 3     #prd=smallos
 4     #typ=386GT
 5     #rel=3.2.2s
 6     #set="The Small OS Product"

 7     uid     root   0
 8     uid     bin    2
 9     gid     root   0
10     gid     bin    2

11     #
12     #!ALL   300     Entire Product
13     #
14     PERM      f644     bin/bin    1    ./etc/perms/smallos        01
15     PERM      f755     bin/bin    1    ./tmp/perms/prep.smallos   01
16     PERM      f755     bin/bin    1    ./tmp/perms/prep.smallos2  01
```

Figure 2-7: Example Permissions List (continued)

```
17    #
18    #!BASEPKG  256     Basic Package
19    #
20    # directory that is part of the required product
21    BASEPKG   d755    bin/bin     1   ./dev
22    # directory not part of the required product (D signifies)
23    BASEPKG   D755    bin/bin     1   ./tmp
24    # standard file
25    BASEPKG   x711    bin/bin     1   ./bin/cat            02
26    # standard file with 3 links
27    BASEPKG   x711    bin/bin     3   ./bin/cp             01
28                                      ./bin/ln             01
29                                      ./bin/mv             01
30    # special chmod bit set, see chmod(BA_OS)
31    BASEPKG   x2111   bin/backup  2   ./bin/df             01
32                                      ./etc/devnm          01
33    # shell script: note that read permissions are needed
34    BASEPKG   f755    bin/bin     1   ./usr/lib/mkdev/lp   02
35    # character device node
36    BASEPKG   c440    root/root   1   ./dev/auditr         21/0

37    #
38    #!DEVPKG   26      Development Package
39    #
40    # block device node
41    DEVPKG    b440    root/bin    1   ./dev/root           1/40
42    # linked device node
43    DEVPKG    c622    root/bin    3   ./dev/console        3/1
44                                      ./dev/syscon
45                                      ./dev/systty
```

Variable Settings

The product name, which is the #prd value in the permissions list, is the pivotal name in the product. Figure 2-8 illustrates how this name is used.

Figure 2-8: Example Product Name Usage

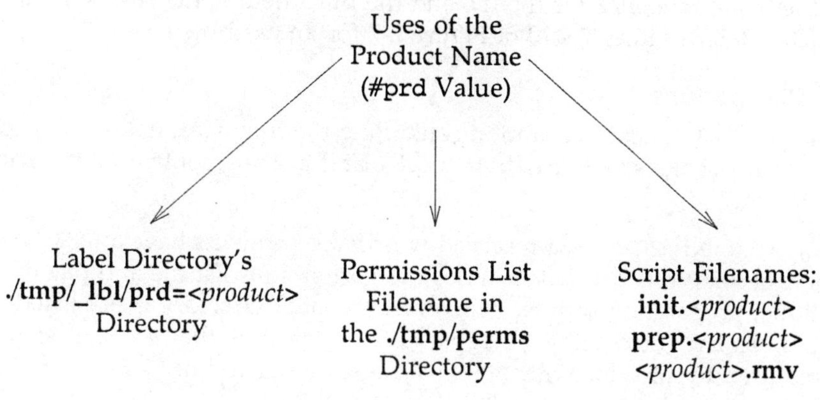

The following values are required and must be in the permissions list file:

- #prd: The product name is the mnemonic name of the product, it is a string of up to eight characters. The #prd value must be the same as the name of the permissions list file. (Refer to line 3 of Figure 2-7 for an example.)

- #set: Used as a verbose product name for user interface display. (Refer to line 6 of Figure 2-7 for an example.)

- #rel: Vendor-defined release string. (Refer to line 5 of Figure 2-7 for an example.)

- #typ: Vendor-defined machine environment string. (Refer to line 4 of Figure 2-7 for an example.)

ID Definitions

User and group ID numbers must be specified at the top of the permissions list file for each user and group mentioned in the file description (described in the "File Descriptions" section that follows). The group ID (gid) values correspond to the information in the /etc/group file. The user ID (uid) values correspond to the information in the /etc/passwd file. The syntax for the definition section is: the first field indicates the type of ID (either "gid" or "uid"), the second field contains the name reference for the ID, and the third field is the corresponding numeric ID. (Refer to lines 7 - 10 of Figure 2-7 for an example.)

Package Declarations

Each package must have a declaration containing the following fields: the package name, the package size in 512-byte blocks, and a string containing the package description.

The package named "PERM" is a reserved word. All products have a PERM package in their permissions list that includes the permissions list file and one or more optional preparation scripts. However, the label directory is not listed in the permissions list. Before the PERM package declaration, the "#! ALL" statement is required to introduce the PERM package. (Refer to lines 12 - 16 of Figure 2-7 for an example.)

Package names must be unique and can be up to 8 characters in length.

File Descriptions

A file description consists of a package specifier, a permission specification, owner and group specifications, the number of links on the file, the file name, and a volume number separated by tabs. (Refer to Figure 2-7, lines 14 through 45 for examples of file descriptions.) The file descriptions fields are:

- **Package specifier** — An arbitrary non-white-space string that is the name of a package within a distribution set. The string length is determined by the remaining number of characters on an 80-column line.

- **Permission specification** — a file type, followed by an octal chmod(BA_OS) permission specification. The file type can be one of the following characters:

a   Archive.

b   Block device.

c   Character device.

d   Directory.

e   Empty file.

f   Data file.

o   Okay. Indicates that there should be no file type checking, allowing any format or contents in what would normally be the header section of an executable. For example, data files should be of type "o".

p   Named pipe.

x   Executable.

If the file type used is an uppercase letter, then the file associated with it is optional. When custom installs a package, it provides a test to ensure that all pieces of the product or package are installed. If a file is not fully installed, custom lists a package or product as "Partially Installed." A product is considered fully installed if:

- The respective permissions list file has been installed into /etc/perms, and

- All required files are installed. A file is designated as required if the file type letter is in lowercase. If the letter is in uppercase, custom does not consider the file as part of the criteria for a complete installation. If all files are installed with uppercase file types, custom evaluates the product as installed only if the permissions list for the product has been installed into /etc/perms.

- **Owner and group specifications** — the owner and group permissions are in the third column separated by a slash: for example, bin/bin. The owner and group names are the same as those defined at the start of the permissions list.

- **Links** — the number of links are in the fourth column. If there are links to the file, the next line contains the linked filename with no preceding information; however, the volume number is required on linked file entries. Linked device nodes do not have volume numbers.

- **File pathname** — the fifth column is the pathname of the file on the distribution media volume and is relative to the root directory. The pathname must be relative (". /"); that is, not preceded by a slash "/".

- **Volume numbers or major-minor numbers** — the sixth column has two uses:

  - The number of the media volume on which a file exists. This column is blank for directories because directories are created as needed when custom executes. The media volume has the same value as the **vol=** directory of the label directory. The maximum number of digits in the volume number is two (up to 99 volumes are possible).

  - Used for special files, giving the major and minor device numbers. After the product files are extracted, custom sets permissions modes and creates the device files. When a device file is linked to another device file, a value is not put in the sixth column of a linked device file entry. See lines 39 through 43 of Figure 2-7 for examples of device file entries.

Configuration Scripts

The three configuration scripts, preparation (**prep**), initialization (**init**), and remove (**rmv**) are called during the custom execution. The scripts can be either shell scripts or executable binaries. The following rules apply to the use of these scripts or binaries:

1. Scripts have defined names. Initialization script filenames have an "init." prefix, preparation script filenames have a "**prep.**" prefix, and remove script filenames have a ".rmv" suffix.

2. The program should trap and handle all error conditions, keeping message writes to the screen to a minimum. Prompts are the exception; initialization scripts generally have prompts to determine configuration information.

3. Scripts are executed by `custom` from the root uid.

4. Return exit codes are 0 (zero) for success or 1 for failure for the initialization and preparation scripts. If 10 is returned, `custom` stops processing immediately. Remove script return codes are ignored.

5. Only the remove script is called with arguments.

Preparation Script

The preparation scripts are executed before any installation activity occurs. Any number of preparation scripts are permitted. The scripts are named with the "**prep.**" prefix. The length of the name following the prefix is limited to eight characters. On the distribution media, the preparation script files are located in the ./tmp/perms directory.

Initialization Script

The initialization scripts are executed after files are extracted from the distribution media during an installation, at the end of a volume being loaded. Initialization scripts must be put at the end of a package.

Any number of initialization scripts are permitted; however, the order in which each script is executed is indeterminate. The scripts are named with the "**init.**" prefix and the length of the name following the prefix is limited to eight characters. On the distribution media, the initialization script files are located in the ./tmp directory. Placing the name of an initialization script in a package associates that script with the package.

Remove Script

The remove script is executed when the product is removed, but before files are removed. The `custom` utility handles the actual removing of files from the selected packages. The remove script should only clean up actions initiated in the initialization and preparation scripts.

One remove script is permitted for a product. The remove script located in the is the same name as the #prd value in the permissions list. When the remove script is executed, it is passed the names of the packages that were selected to be removed with each argument separated by a space. If all packages are selected to be removed, a single argument "ALL" is passed to the remove script.

File Tree for Add-on Software

/etc/perms and /usr/lib/custom are reserved in the file tree for the installation of application software packages. Each add-on software package should adhere to the following rules:

- The permissions list file will be installed into /etc/perms with the name *product* by custom, where <*product*> is the same name as the #prd value in the permissions list.

- The remove script will be installed into /usr/lib/custom with the name <*product*>.rmv by custom, where <*product*> is the same name as the #prd value in the permissions list.

Commands that Install, Remove and Access Packages

The custom installation utility is used to install, remove, and access packages. The custom utility has these attributes:

- The custom utility is invoked from the command line by entering "custom." When invoked, the utility can be operated in either interactive mode or in non-interactive mode. When used in non-interactive mode, the utility has this format:

```
custom -a product-to-add
custom -f install-file
custom -i install-package(s)
custom -l list-package(s)
custom -r remove-package(s)
```

Each of these options is mutually exclusive. If any information
is missing from the command line, custom prompts for the
missing data. The –m flag allows the media device to be
specified. The default is **/dev/install**.

■ The custom utility installs, lists, or removes the software product, as a
complete unit, by package (groups of files), or by individual files.

■ The custom utility interprets the permissions list to determine the order
in which files and packages are to be installed or removed. It uses the
information in the permissions list to create device files for block and
character devices and directories.

■ The custom utility displays the size of previously installed packages in
512-byte blocks. It also displays the sizes of packages to be installed.

■ The custom utility displays which products are installed.

■ The custom utility executes the previously described preparation, initialization, and remove scripts. The scripts are invoked with the
popen(BA_OS) function and can be either shell scripts or executable programs.

■ The custom utility removes permissions lists when "ALL" packages are
selected to be removed.

3 LOW-LEVEL SYSTEM INFORMATION

Introduction   3-1

Character Representations   3-2

Machine Interface   3-3
Processor Architecture   3-3
Data Representation   3-4
- Fundamental Types   3-4
- Aggregates and Unions   3-5
- Bit-Fields   3-8
Memory Synchronization   3-11

Function Calling Sequence   3-14
Registers and the Stack Frame   3-14
Functions Returning Scalars or No Value   3-19
Functions Returning Structures or Unions   3-21
Integral and Pointer Arguments   3-24
Floating-Point Arguments   3-24
Structure and Union Arguments   3-25

Operating System Interface   3-27
Virtual Address Space   3-27
- Page Size   3-27
- Virtual Address Assignments   3-27
- Managing the Process Stack   3-29

System Call Interface 3-30
- Future Directions 3-37

Exception Interface 3-37
- Hardware Exception Types 3-37
- Software Trap Types 3-39
- Signal Stack 3-39
- Future Directions 3-44

Process Initialization 3-44
- Special Registers 3-44
- Process Stack and Registers 3-46

Coding Examples 3-50

Data Objects 3-50
Function Calls 3-52
Parameter Passing 3-53
Branching 3-55
C Stack Frame 3-56
Variable Argument List 3-58
Allocating Stack Space Dynamically 3-59
Allocating Heap Space Dynamically 3-61
Identifying the Processor 3-61

Introduction

This chapter defines low-level system information, much of which is processor-specific. It gives the constraints imposed by the system on application programs, and it describes how application programs use operating system services.

ANSI C serves as the iBCS reference programming language. By defining the implementation of C data types, the iBCS can give precise system interface information without resorting to assembly language. Giving C language bindings for system services does *not* preclude binding for other programming languages. Moreover, the examples given here are not intended to specify the C language available on the system.

According to ANSI C, a bit-field may have type `int`, `unsigned int`, or `signed int`. The C language used in this iBCS allows bit-fields of type `char`, `short`, `int`, and `long` (plus their `signed` and `unsigned` variants), and of type `enum`.

This chapter's major sections discuss the following topics.

Character representations.
> This section defines the standard character set used for external files that should be portable among systems.

Machine interface.
> This section describes the processor architecture available to application programs. It also defines the reference language data types, giving the foundation for system interface specifications.

Function calling sequence.
> This section describes the standard function calling sequence that accommodates the operating system interface, including system calls, signals, and stack management.

Operating system interface.
> This section describes the operating system mechanisms that are visible to application programs (such as signals, process initialization, etc.).

Character Representations

Several external file formats represent control information with characters (for example, see "Archive File" in Chapter 7). These single-byte characters use the 7-bit ASCII character set. In other words, when the iBCS mentions character constants, such as '/' or '\n', their numerical values should follow the 7-bit ASCII guidelines. For the previous character constants, the single-byte values would be decimal 47 and 10 respectively.

Character values outside the range of 0 to 127 may occupy one or more bytes, according to the character encoding. Applications can control their own character sets, using different character set extensions for different languages as appropriate. Although iBCS-conformance does not restrict the character sets, they generally should follow some simple guidelines.

- Character values between 0 and 127 should correspond to the 7-bit ASCII code. That is, character sets with encodings above 127 should include the 7-bit ASCII code as a subset.

- The first byte in a non-ASCII multibyte character should be outside the range of 0 to 127. Secondary bytes in a multibyte character should be encoded such that a byte resembling a 7-bit ASCII character is not "embed" within a multibyte, non-ASCII character.

- Multibyte characters should be self-identifying. This allows, for example, any multibyte character to be inserted between any pair of multibyte characters, without changing the characters' interpretations.

These cautions are particularly relevant for multilingual applications.

Machine Interface

Processor Architecture

The Intel *80386 Programmer's Reference Manual* (Intel Literature order number 230985) and the Intel *80387 Programmer's Reference Manual* (Intel Literature order number 231917) together define the processor architecture. The architecture of the combined Intel386 processor and Intel387™ coprocessors is hereafter referred to as the Intel386 architecture. The Intel *i486™ MICROPROCESSOR Programmer's Reference Manual* (Intel Literature order number 240486) defines a compatible member of the Intel386 processor architecture family. Programs intended to execute directly on the processor use the instruction set, instruction encodings, and instruction semantics of the architecture. Three points deserve explicit mention:

- A program may assume all documented instructions exist.

- A program may assume all documented instructions work.

- A program may use only the instructions defined by the architecture.

In other words, from a program's perspective, the execution environment provides a complete and working implementation of the Intel386 architecture.

This does not imply that the underlying implementation provides all instructions in hardware, only that the instructions perform the specified operations and produce the specified results. The iBCS neither places performance constraints on systems nor specifies what instructions must be implemented in hardware. A software emulation of the architecture could conform to the iBCS.

Some processors might support the Intel386 architecture as a subset, providing additional instructions or capabilities. Programs that use those capabilities explicitly do not conform to the iBCS. Executing those programs on machines without the additional capabilities gives undefined behavior.

Data Representation

Within this specification, the term *halfword* refers to a 16-bit object, the term *word* refers to a 32-bit object, and the term *doubleword* refers to a 64-bit object.

Fundamental Types

Figure 3-1 shows the correspondence between ANSI C's scalar types and the processor's data types.

Figure 3-1: Scalar Types

Type	C	sizeof	Alignment (bytes)	Intel386 Architecture
Integral	char signed char	1	1	signed byte
	unsigned char	1	1	unsigned byte
	short signed short	2	2	signed halfword
	unsigned short	2	2	unsigned halfword
	int signed int long signed long enum	4	4	signed word
	unsigned int unsigned long	4	4	unsigned word
Pointer	*any-type* * *any-type* (*)()	4	4	unsigned word
Floating-point	float	4	4	single-precision (IEEE)
	double	8	4	double-precision (IEEE)
	long double	12	4	extended-precision (IEEE)

 The Intel386 architecture does not require doubleword alignment for double-precision values. Nevertheless, for data structure compatibility with other Intel architectures, compilers may provide a method to align double-precision values on doubleword boundaries.

 A compiler that provides the doubleword alignment mentioned in the previous note can generate code (data structures and function calling sequences) that does not conform to the iBCS. Programs built with the doubleword alignment facility can thus violate conformance to the iBCS. See "Aggregates and Unions" and "Function Calling Sequence" later in this chapter for more information.

A null pointer (for all types) has the value zero.

The `long double` data type only occupies the first 10-bytes of the 12-bytes allocated, according to the Intel387 coprocessor format. The last two bytes are padded with undefined values.

The Intel386 architecture does not require all data access to be properly aligned, nor does it require data objects to be properly aligned the same as their size. For example, double-precision values occupy 1 doubleword (8-bytes), and their natural alignment is a word boundary, meaning their addresses are multiples of 4. Compilers should allocate independent data objects with the proper alignment; examples include global arrays of double-precision variables, FORTRAN COMMON blocks, and unconstrained stack objects. However, some language facilities (such as FORTRAN EQUIVALENCE statements) may create objects with only byte alignment. Consequently, arbitrary data accesses, such as pointer dereference or reference arguments, might or might not be properly aligned. Accessing misaligned data will be slower than accessing properly aligned data, but otherwise there is no difference.

Aggregates and Unions

Aggregates (structures and arrays) and unions assume the alignment of their most strictly aligned component. The size of any object, including aggregates and unions, is always a multiple of the object's alignment. An array uses the same alignment as its elements. Structure and union objects can require padding to meet size and alignment constraints. The contents of any padding is undefined.

- An entire structure or union object is aligned on the same boundary as its most strictly aligned member.

- Each member is assigned to the lowest available offset with the appropriate alignment. This may require *internal padding*, depending on the previous member.

- A structure's size is increased, if necessary, to make it a multiple of the alignment. This may require *tail padding*, depending on the last member.

In the following examples, members' byte offsets appear in the upper right corners.

Figure 3-2: Structure Smaller Than a Word

```
struct {
    char    c;
};
```

Byte aligned, sizeof is 1

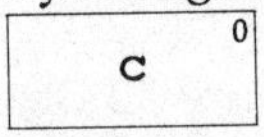

c [0]

Figure 3-3: No Padding

```
struct {
    char    c;
    char    d;
    short   s;
    long    n;
};
```

Word aligned, sizeof is 8

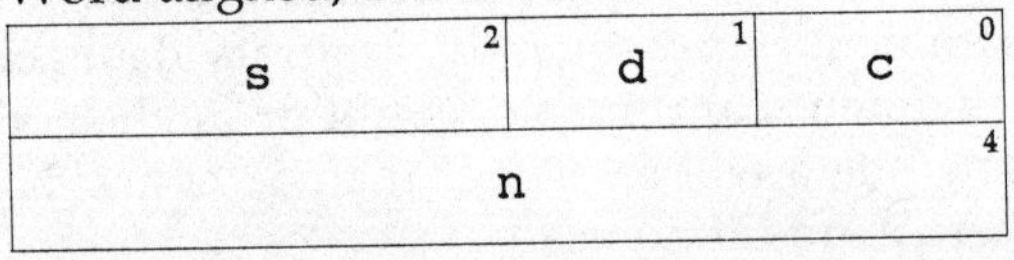

s [2]	d [1]	c [0]
n [4]		

Figure 3-4: Internal Padding

```
struct {
    char    c;
    short   s;
};
```

Halfword aligned, sizeof is 4

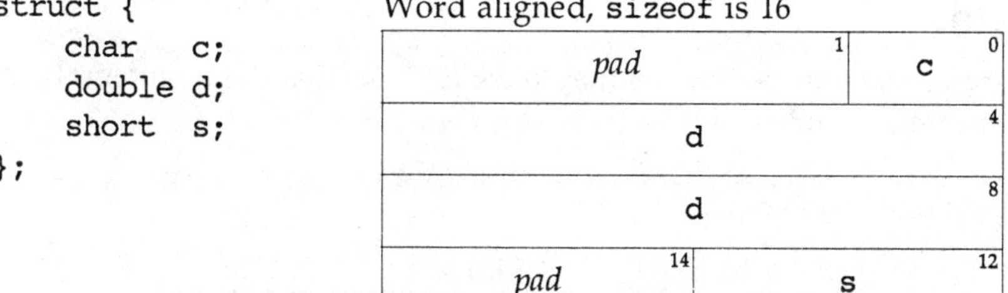

Figure 3-5: Internal and Tail Padding

```
struct {
    char    c;
    double  d;
    short   s;
};
```

Word aligned, sizeof is 16

 NOTE	The Intel386 architecture does not require doubleword alignment for double-precision values. Nevertheless, for data structure compatibility with other Intel architectures, compilers may provide a method to align double-precision values on doubleword boundaries.

CAUTION	A compiler that provides the doubleword alignment mentioned in the previous note would arrange the preceding structure differently. Programs built with the doubleword alignment facility may not conform to the iBCS, and they may not be data-compatible with conforming Intel386 programs.

Figure 3-6: union **Allocation**

```
union {
    char   c;
    short  s;
    int    j;
};
```

Word aligned, sizeof is 4

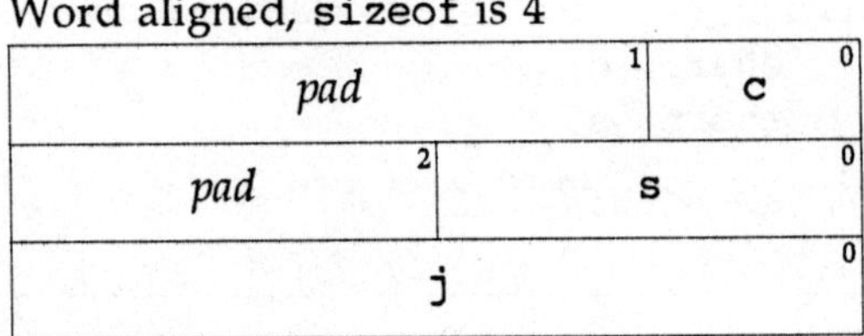

Bit-Fields

C struct and union definitions may have *bit-fields* that define integral objects
with a specified number of bits.

Figure 3-7: Bit-Field Ranges

Bit-field Type	Width w	Range
signed char		-2^{w-1} to $2^{w-1}-1$
char	1 to 8	0 to $2^{w}-1$
unsigned char		0 to $2^{w}-1$
signed short		-2^{w-1} to $2^{w-1}-1$
short	1 to 16	0 to $2^{w}-1$
unsigned short		0 to $2^{w}-1$
signed int		-2^{w-1} to $2^{w-1}-1$
int		0 to $2^{w}-1$
enum	1 to 32	0 to $2^{w}-1$
unsigned int		0 to $2^{w}-1$
signed long		-2^{w-1} to $2^{w-1}-1$
long	1 to 32	0 to $2^{w}-1$
unsigned long		0 to $2^{w}-1$

"Plain" bit-fields (that is, those neither signed nor unsigned) always have
non-negative values. Although they may have type char, short, int, or long
(which can have negative values), these bit-fields have the same range as a bit-
field of the same size with the corresponding unsigned type. Bit-fields obey
the same size and alignment rules as other structure and union members, with
the following additions:

- Bit-fields are allocated from right to left (least to most significant).

- A bit-field must entirely reside in a storage unit appropriate for its
  declared type. Thus a bit-field never crosses its unit boundary.

- Bit-fields may share a storage unit with other struct/union members,
  including members that are not bit-fields. Of course, struct members
  occupy different parts of the storage unit.

- Unnamed bit-fields' types do not affect the alignment of a structure or
  union, although individual bit-fields' member offsets obey the alignment
  constraints.

The following examples show struct and union members' byte offsets in the
upper right corners; bit numbers appear in the lower corners.

Figure 3-8: Bit Numbering

0x01020304	01	02	03	04

Figure 3-9: Right-to-Left Allocation

```
struct {
    int     j:5;
    int     k:6;
    int     m:7;
};
```

Word aligned, sizeof is 4

pad	m	k	j

Figure 3-10: Boundary Alignment

```
struct {
    short   s:9;
    int     j:9;
    char    c;
    short   t:9;
    short   u:9;
    char    d;
};
```

Word aligned, sizeof is 12

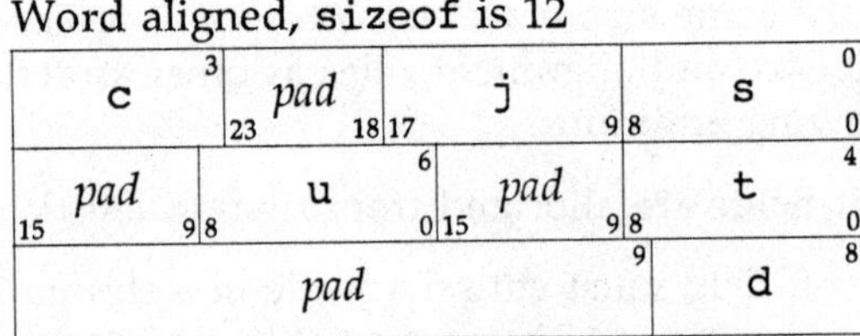

Figure 3-11: Storage Unit Sharing

```
struct {
    char    c;
    short   s:8;
};
```

Halfword aligned, sizeof is 2

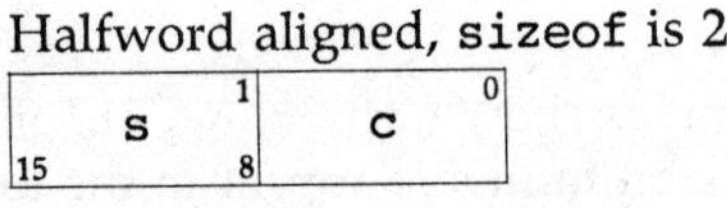

Figure 3-12: union Allocation

```
union {
    char    c;
    short   s:8;
};
```

Halfword aligned, sizeof is 2

Figure 3-13: Unnamed Bit-Fields

```
struct {
    char    c;
    int     :0;
    char    d;
    short   :9;
    char    e;
    char    :0;
};
```

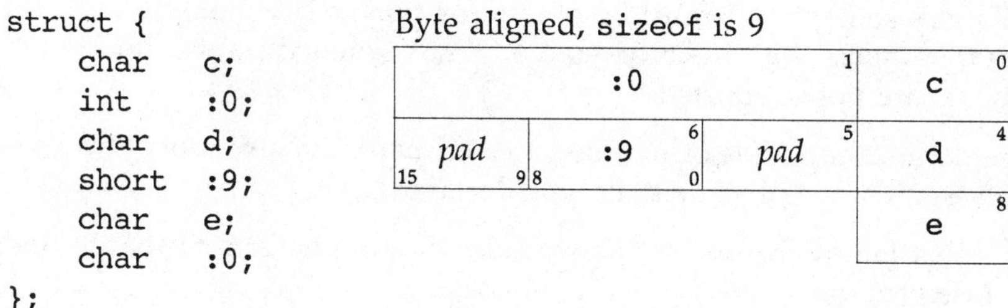

As the examples show, `int` bit-fields (including `signed` and `unsigned`) pack
more densely than smaller base types. One can use `char` and `short` bit-fields
to force particular alignments, but `int` is generally more efficient.

Memory Synchronization

Applications may use shared memory for communication and synchronization
between processes. Application code that uses memory semaphores for synchronization of critical sections must observe the following rules:

- Memory semaphores must be altered (both set and cleared) with atomic
  instructions. See the Intel *80386 Programmer's Reference Manual* (Intel
  Literature order number 230985) or the Intel *i486™ MICROPROCESSOR
  Programmer's Reference Manual* (Intel Literature order number 240486) for a
  description of atomic instructions.

- Modifications of the memory semaphores must use the `lock` instruction
  prefix on an instruction that is compatible with the `lock`; otherwise the
  `xchg` instruction can be used instead. The `xchg` instruction asserts the
  `lock` semantics implicitly, and so can be used without the `lock` prefix.

- Memory semaphores can be read with ordinary memory access instructions.

■ Memory semaphores must be properly aligned, that is, a semaphore can not cross a word boundary.

■ Memory semaphores must be of integral type, e.g., `char`, `short`, `int`, `long` or `enum`, with their `signed` and `unsigned` variants. Bit-field semaphores are not supported.

■ Memory semaphores cannot be accessed partially, and must always be accessed using the same data type declaration.

Programs that fail to observe the above rules do not conform to the iBCS. Executing those programs gives undefined behavior.

Figure 3-14 illustrates the proper ways to set a memory semaphore.

Figure 3-14: Setting Memory Semaphore

```
        lock                            / lock prefix
        incl    mem_lock                / increment semaphore

or

        movl    $1,%eax                 / new value
        xchgl   %eax,mem_lock           / set and read semaphore
```

Figure 3-15 illustrates the proper ways to clear a memory semaphore.

Figure 3-15: Clearing Memory Semaphore

```
        lock                        / lock prefix
        decl    mem_lock            / decrement semaphore

        or

        movl    $0,%eax             / clear value
        xchgl   %eax,mem_lock       / clear and read semaphore
```

Any of the instructions from the Intel386 architecture that are compatible with the `lock` instruction prefix can be used in placed of the `inc` and `dec` instructions in the above examples.

Figure 3-16 shows how a test-and-set spinlock should be implemented. This sequence is designed to minimize interference with overall system performance in a multiprocessor system.

Figure 3-16: Test-and-Set Spinlock

```
lock_busy:
        movl    mem_lock,%eax       / get semaphore
        orl     %eax,%eax           / test semaphore
        jnz     lock_busy           / spin if busy
        movl    $1,%eax             / lock value
        xchgl   %eax,mem_lock       / set & read semaphore
        orl     %eax,%eax           / test semaphore
        jnz     lock_busy           / spin if busy
```

Function Calling Sequence

This section discusses the standard function calling sequence, including stack frame layout, register usage, parameter passing, etc. The system libraries described in Chapter 6 require this calling sequence.

The standard calling sequence *requirements* apply only to global functions. Local functions that are not reachable from other compilation units may use different conventions. Nonetheless, it is recommended that all functions use the standard calling sequence when possible.

C programs follow the conventions given here. For specific information on the implementation of C, see "Coding Examples" in this chapter. Programs in other languages may have slightly different conventions, but the C program conventions must be followed when calling external functions because the system libraries require this calling sequence.

Registers and the Stack Frame

The Intel386 architecture provides a number of registers. All the integer registers and all the floating-point registers are global to all procedures in a running program.

Brief register descriptions appear in Figure 3-17, more complete information appears later.

Figure 3-17: Processor Registers

Type	Name	Usage
General	%eax	Return value
	%edx	Dividend register (divide operations)
	%ecx	Count register (shift and string operations)
	%ebx	Local register variable
	%ebp	Stack frame pointer
	%esi	Local register variable
	%edi	Local register variable
	%esp	Stack pointer
Floating-point	%st(0)	floating-point stack top, return value
	%st(1)	floating-point next to stack top
	. . .	
	%st(7)	floating-point stack bottom

In addition to registers, each function has a frame on the run-time stack. This stack grows downward from high addresses. Figure 3-18 shows the stack frame organization.

Figure 3-18: Standard Stack Frame

Position	Contents	Frame	
			High addresses
	. . .		
$4n+8$(%ebp)	argument word n		
	. . .	Previous	
8(%ebp)	argument word 0		
4(%ebp)	return address		
0(%ebp)	previous %ebp		
−4(%ebp)	unspecified		
	. . .		
	variable size	Current	
	optional		
	register variable		
0(%esp)	save area		
	. . .		
			Low addresses

Several key points about the stack frame deserve mention.

- The stack frame is word aligned. Although the architecture does not require any alignment of the stack, software convention and the operating system requires the stack to be aligned on a word boundary.

- Argument words are pushed onto the stack in reverse order (that is, the rightmost argument in C call syntax has the highest address), preserving the stack's word alignment. All incoming arguments appear on the stack, residing in the stack frame of the caller.

- An argument's size is increased, if necessary, to make it a multiple of words. This may require tail padding, depending on the size of the argument.

- The optional register variable save area is present only if the compiler chooses to save registers that are used within the function in this area, and it may range in size from zero to three words. A compiler may choose to save its registers anywhere within the stack frame; but some compiler will save the registers in this register variable save area, and the position of these values relative to the stack pointer must be preserved by any function that modifies the `%esp` register.

- Other areas depend on the compiler and the code being compiled. The standard calling sequence does not define a maximum stack frame size, nor does it restrict how a language system uses the "unspecified" area of the standard stack frame.

All registers on the Intel386 architecture are global and thus visible to both a calling and a called function. Registers `%esp`, `%ebp`, `%ebx`, `%edi`, and `%esi` "belong" to the calling function. In other words, a called function must preserve these registers' values for its caller. Remaining registers "belong" to the called function. If a calling function wants to preserve such a register value across a function call, it must save the value in its local stack frame.

Some registers have assigned roles in the standard calling sequence:

`%esp`	The *stack pointer* holds the limit of the current stack frame, which is the address of the stack's bottom-most, valid word. At all times, the stack pointer must point to a word-aligned area. Except in the case of dynamic stack allocation, this register is preserved across any functions called by the current function. A called function that does not preserve the stack pointer must notify the compiler, which must generate code that behaves properly. Failure to notify the compiler leads to undefined behavior. The standard function calling sequence does not include any methods to detect such failures.
	Because the stack pointer is preserved for the caller, the arguments that are pushed on the stack are still present upon return from any function call; it is the responsibility of the caller to adjust the stack pointer to pop off the arguments.
`%ebp`	The *frame pointer* holds a base address for the current stack frame. Consequently, a function has registers pointing to both ends of its frame. Incoming arguments reside in the previous frame, referenced as positive offsets from `%ebp`, while local variables reside in the current frame, referenced as negative offsets from `%ebp`. A called function must preserve this register's value for its caller.

%eax   *Integral and pointer return values* appear in %eax. A function that returns a struct or union value places the address of the result in %eax. Otherwise this is a scratch register.

%ebx, %esi and %edi

These *local registers* have no specified role in the function calling sequence. A called function must preserve their values for the caller.

%ecx and %edx   *Scratch registers* have no specified role in the standard calling sequence. Called functions do not have to preserve their values for the caller.

%st(0)   *Floating-point return values* appear on the top of the floating-point register stack; there is no difference in the representation of single- or double-precision values in floating-point registers. If the function does not return a floating-point value, then this register must be empty. This register must be empty before entry to a function.

%st(1) through %st(7)

Floating-point scratch registers have no specified role in the standard calling sequence. These registers must be empty before entry to and upon exit from a function.

EFLAGS   The *flags register* contains the system flags, such as the direction flag and the carry flag. The direction flag must be set to the "forward" (that is, zero) direction before entry to and upon exit from a function. Other user flags have no specified role in the standard calling sequence and are not preserved.

Floating-Point Control Word

The Intel387 coprocessor *control word* contains the floating-point flags, such as the rounding mode and exception masking. This register is initialized at process initialization time to a specific value. The called function must preserve the pre-initialized fields in this register. Failure to preserve this register may lead to undefined behavior. The standard function calling sequence does not include any method to detect such failures.

Signals can interrupt processes [see `signal(BA_OS)`]. Functions called during signal handling have no unusual restrictions on their use of registers. Moreover, if a signal handling function returns, the process resumes its original execution path with registers restored to their original values. Thus, programs and compilers may freely use all registers without the danger of signal handlers changing their values.

Functions Returning Scalars or No Value

A function that returns an integral or pointer value places its result in register `%eax`.

A floating-point return value appears on the top of the Intel387 coprocessor register stack. The caller then must remove the value from the Intel387 coprocessor stack, even if it doesn't use the value. Failure of either side to meet its obligations leads to undefined program behavior. The standard calling sequence does not include any method to detect such failures nor to detect return value type mismatches. Therefore the user must declare all functions properly. There is no difference in the representation of single-, double- or extended-precision values in floating-point registers.

Functions that return no value (also called procedures or `void` functions) put no particular value in any register.

A `call` instruction pushes the address of the next instruction (the return address) onto the stack. The `ret` instruction pops the address off the stack and effectively continues execution at the next instruction after the `call` instruction. A function that returns a scalar or no value must preserve the caller's registers as described earlier. Additionally, the called function must remove the return address from the stack, leaving the stack pointer (`%esp`) with the value it had before the `call` instruction was executed.

Figure 3-19 shows a function prologue that allocates 80 bytes of local stack space and saves the local registers `%ebx`, `%esi`, and `%edi`.

Figure 3-19: Function Prologue

```
prologue:
        pushl   %ebp            / save frame pointer
        movl    %esp, %ebp      / set new frame pointer
        subl    $80, %esp       / allocate stack space
        pushl   %edi            / save local register
        pushl   %esi            / save local register
        pushl   %ebx            / save local register
```

Figure 3-20 shows an epilogue for the example that restores the state for the caller. This example returns the value in %edi by moving it to %eax.

Figure 3-20: Function Epilogue

```
        movl    %edi, %eax      / set up return value
epilogue:
        popl    %ebx            / restore local register
        popl    %esi            / restore local register
        popl    %edi            / restore local register
        movl    %ebp,%esp       / restore stack pointer
        popl    %ebp            / restore frame pointer
        ret                     / pop return address
```

NOTE Although some functions can be optimized to eliminate the save and restore of the frame pointer, the general case uses the standard prologue and epilogue.

Sections below describe where arguments appear on the stack. The examples are written as if the function prologue described in 9 had been used.

Functions Returning Structures or Unions

If a function returns a structure or union, then the caller provides space for the return value and places its address on the stack as argument word zero. In effect, this address becomes a "hidden" first argument. Having the caller supply the return object's space allows re-entrancy.

NOTE Structures and unions in this context have fixed sizes. The iBCS does not specify how to handle variable sized objects.

A function that returns a structure or union also sets %eax to the value of the original address of the caller's area before it returns. Thus when the caller receives control again, the address of the returned object resides in register %eax and can be used to access the object. Both the calling and the called functions must cooperate to pass the return value successfully:

- The calling function must supply space for the return value and pass its address in the stack frame;

- The called function must use the address from the frame and copy the return value to the object so supplied;

- The called function must remove this address from the stack before returning.

Failure of either side to meet its obligations leads to undefined program behavior. The standard function calling sequence does not include any method to detect such failures nor to detect structure and union type mismatches. Therefore the user must declare all functions properly.

Figure 3-21 illustrates the stack contents when the function receives control
(after the `call` instruction) and when the calling function again receives control
(after the `ret` instruction).

Figure 3-21: Stack Contents for Functions Returning `struct/union`

Position	After call	After ret	Position
$4n+4$(`%esp`)	argument word n	argument word n	$4n-4$(`%esp`)
	. . .	. . .	
8(`%esp`)	argument word 1	argument word 1	0(`%esp`)
4(`%esp`)	value address	*undefined*	
0(`%esp`)	return address		

To illustrate, the function prologue in Figure 3-22 allocates 80 bytes of local
stack space and saves the local registers `%ebx`, `%esi`, and `%edi`. Additionally, it
removes the "hidden" argument from the stack and saves it in the highest word
of the local stack frame.

Figure 3-22: Function Prologue (Returning `struct/union`**)**

```
prologue:
    popl    %eax            / pop return address
    xchgl   %eax, 0(%esp)   / swap return address
                            / and return value address
    pushl   %ebp            / save frame pointer
    movl    %esp, %ebp      / set new frame pointer
    subl    $80, %esp       / allocate local space
    pushl   %edi            / save local register
    pushl   %esi            / save local register
    pushl   %ebx            / save local register
    movl    %eax, -4(%ebp)      / save return value address
```

Figure 3-23 shows an epilogue for the example that restores the state for the caller.

Figure 3-23: Function Epilogue

```
        movl    -4(%ebp), %eax      / set up return value
epilogue:
        popl    %ebx            / restore local register
        popl    %esi            / restore local register
        popl    %edi            / restore local register
        movl    %ebp,%esp       / restore stack pointer
        popl    %ebp            / restore frame pointer
        ret                     / pop return address
```

Although some functions can be optimized to eliminate the save and restore of the frame pointer, the general case uses the standard prologue and epilogue.

Sections below describe where arguments appear on the stack. The examples are written as if the function prologue described in Figure 3-22 had been used.

Integral and Pointer Arguments

As mentioned, a function receives all its arguments through the stack; the last argument is pushed first. In the standard calling sequence, the first argument is at offset `8(%ebp)`, the second argument is at offset `12(%ebp)`, etc. as shown in Figure 3-24. Functions pass all integer-valued arguments as words, sign-extending signed or zero-extending unsigned bytes and halfwords as needed.

Figure 3-24: Integral and Pointer Arguments

Call	Argument	Stack address
	1	`8(%ebp)`
`g(1, 2, 3,`	2	`12(%ebp)`
`(void *)0);`	3	`16(%ebp)`
	`(void *)0`	`20(%ebp)`

Floating-Point Arguments

The stack also holds floating-point arguments: single-precision values use one word, double-precision use two, and extended-precision use three. See "Coding Examples" for information about floating-point arguments and variable argument lists. The example in Figure 3-25 uses only double-precision arguments. Single- and extended-precision arguments behave as specified earlier.

Figure 3-25: Floating-Point Arguments

Call	Argument	Stack address
h(1.414, 1, 2.998e10);	word 0, 1.414	8(%ebp)
	word 1, 1.414	12(%ebp)
	1	16(%ebp)
	word 0, 2.998e10	20(%ebp)
	word 1, 2.998e10	24(%ebp)

NOTE The Intel386 architecture does not require doubleword alignment for double-precision values. Nevertheless, for data structure compatibility with other Intel architectures, compilers may provide a method to align double-precision values on doubleword boundaries.

CAUTION A compiler that provides the doubleword alignment mentioned in the previous note would have to maintain doubleword alignment for the stack. Moreover, the arguments in the preceding example would appear in different positions. Programs built with the doubleword alignment facility may not conform to the iBCS, and their function calling sequence may not be compatible with conforming Intel386 programs.

Structure and Union Arguments

As described earlier in the data representation section, structures and unions can have byte, halfword, or word alignment, depending on the constituents. An argument's size is increased, if necessary, to make it a multiple of words. This may require tail padding, depending on the size of the argument. To ensure that data in the stack is properly aligned, the stack pointer must always point to a word boundary. Structure and union arguments are pushed onto the stack in the same manner as integral arguments, described earlier. This provides call-by-value semantics, letting the called function modify its arguments without affecting the calling function's object. Figure 3-26 shows an example of a structure argument.

Figure 3-26: Structure and Union Arguments

Call	Argument	Callee
i(1, s);	1 word 0, s word 1, s ...	8(%ebp) 12(%ebp) 16(%ebp) ...

Virtual Address Space

Processes execute in a 32-bit virtual address space. Memory management
hardware translates virtual addresses to physical addresses, hiding physical
addressing and letting a process run anywhere in the system's real memory.
Processes typically begin with three logical segments, commonly called text,
data, and stack. As Chapters 4 and 5 describe, shared libraries can create additional segments for themselves with system services.

Page Size

Memory is organized by pages, which are the system's smallest units of
memory allocation. The page size for the Intel386 architecture is 4 KB.

Virtual Address Assignments

Conceptually, processes have the full 32-bit address space available. In practice,
however, several factors limit the size of a process.

- The system reserves a configuration-dependent amount of virtual space.

- The system limits the process size through a tunable configuration parameter.

- A process whose size exceeds the system's available, combined physical
  memory and secondary storage cannot run. Although some physical
  memory must be present to run any process, the system can execute
  processes that are bigger than physical memory, paging them to and from
  secondary storage. Nonetheless, both physical memory and secondary
  storage are shared resources. System load, which can vary from one program execution to the next, affects the available amounts.

Figure 3-27 illustrates the virtual address configuration.

Figure 3-27: Virtual Address Configuration

<table>
<tr><td>0xffffffff</td><td>Reserved</td><td>End of memory</td></tr>
<tr><td></td><td>. . .</td><td></td></tr>
<tr><td></td><td>. . .</td><td></td></tr>
<tr><td></td><td>Stack and
Dynamic segments</td><td></td></tr>
<tr><td></td><td>. . .</td><td></td></tr>
<tr><td></td><td>Reserved</td><td></td></tr>
<tr><td></td><td>. . .</td><td></td></tr>
<tr><td>0</td><td>Loadable segments</td><td>Beginning of memory</td></tr>
</table>

Programs that dereference null pointers are erroneous. Although such programs may appear to work on the Intel386 architecture, they might fail or behave differently on other systems. To enhance portability, programmers are strongly cautioned not to rely on this behavior.

Loadable segments   Processes' loadable segments may begin at 0. The exact addresses depend on the executable file format [see further information below and in Chapters 4 and 5].

Stack and dynamic segments

A process's stack and dynamic segments reside below the reserved area. Processes can control the amount of virtual memory allotted for stack space, as described below.

Reserved   A reserved area resides at the top of virtual space; processes may not establish address mappings in this area.

As Figure 3-27 shows, the system reserves the high end of virtual address space, with a process's stack and dynamic segments below that. Although the exact boundary between the reserved area and a process depends on the system's configuration, the reserved area shall not consume more than half of the virtual address space. Thus, the user virtual address range has a minimum upper bound of 0x7fffffff. Individual systems may reserve less space, increasing processes' virtual memory range. More information follows in the section ''Managing the Process Stack.''

Although applications may control their memory assignments, the typical arrangement follows the diagram in Figure 3-27. Loadable segments reside at low addresses; dynamic segments occupy the higher range. When applications let the system choose addresses for dynamic segments (such as shared library segments), it chooses high addresses. This leaves the ''middle'' of the address spectrum available for dynamic memory allocation with facilities such as malloc(BA_OS).

Processes must *not* depend on finding their dynamic segments at particular virtual addresses. Facilities exist to let the system choose dynamic segment virtual addresses. The stack resides immediately below the dynamic segments, growing toward lower addresses.

Managing the Process Stack

The section ''Process Initialization'' in this chapter describes the initial stack contents. Stack addresses can change from one system to the next — even from one process execution to the next on the same system. A process, therefore, must not depend on finding its stack at a particular virtual address.

The stack segment has read and write permissions.

A tunable configuration parameter controls the system maximum stack size. Changes in the stack virtual address and size affect the virtual addresses for dynamic segments; consequently, processes must not depend on finding their dynamic segments at particular virtual addresses. Facilities exist to let the system choose dynamic-segment virtual addresses.

System Call Interface

This section on system call interface details is at Level 2.

Four execution modes exist in the Intel386 architecture: ring 3 (or user mode) and three privileged rings. User processes run in user mode (the least privileged). The operating system kernel runs in a privileged mode ring, although the iBCS does not specify which one. A program executes the `lcall` instruction through a system call gate to change execution modes, and thus the `lcall` instruction provides the low-level interface to system calls.

A system call template appears in Figure 3-28.

Figure 3-28: System Call Template

```
name:
        movl    $syscall_number,%eax
        lcall   $0x7,$0
        jc      .L0
        xorl    %eax,%eax
        ret
.L0:
        movl    %eax,errno
        movl    $-1,%eax
        ret
```

Though individual system calls may vary, this template illustrates the following common characteristics:

■ This template expects to receive control with a stack frame as described in "Function Calling Sequence," earlier in this chapter. Consequently, arguments reside on the stack: `4(%esp)` for the initial word, `8(%esp)` for the next word, and so on, before the `lcall` instruction. See the **SVID** for specifications of system call arguments and semantics.

■ Before the `lcall` instruction, register `%eax` must hold the system call number. The correspondence between numbers and system calls appears in Figure 3-29.

■ The `lcall` instruction transfers control to the operating system to perform the desired service.

■ When an error occurs, the operating system sets the carry flag in the processor EFLAGS register and places the error number in register `%eax`.

■ Otherwise, the system call completed successfully, the carry flag will be zero, and the `jc` (jump on carry) instruction will not jump to the error handling code. System call return values appear in registers `%eax` and `%edx`.

Figure 3-29 is a list of the system calls with their numbers in decimal. All other unlisted system call numbers are reserved, programs that use any system call not listed below do not conform to the iBCS.

Figure 3-29: System Call Numbers (in decimal)

access	33
acct	51
alarm	27
brk	17
chdir	12
chmod	15
chown	16
chroot	61
close	6
creat	8
dup	41
exec	11
execve	59
exit	1
fcntl	62

Figure 3-29: System Call Numbers (in decimal) (continued)

fork	2
fpathconf	12072
fstat	28
fstatfs	38
getdents	81
getegid	47
geteuid	24
getgid	47
getgroups	11048
getmsg	85
getpgrp	39
getpid	20
getppid	20
getuid	24
gtty	32
ioctl	54
kill	37
link	9
lseek	19
mkdir	80
mknod	14
mount	21
msgctl	49
msgget	49
msgrcv	49
msgsnd	49
nice	34
open	5
pathconf	11816
pause	29
pipe	42
plock	45
poll	87
profil	44
ptrace	26
putmsg	86
read	3

Figure 3-29: System Call Numbers (in decimal) (continued)

rename	12328
rmdir	79
sbrk	17
semctl	53
semget	53
semop	53
setgid	46
setgroups	11304
setpgid	39
setpgrp	39
setsid	39
setuid	23
shmat	52
shmctl	52
shmdt	52
shmget	52
sigaction	10024
sighold	48
sigignore	48
signal	48
sigpause	48
sigpending	10536
sigprocmask	10280
sigrelse	48
sigset	48
sigsuspend	10792
stat	18
statfs	35
stime	25
stty	31
sync	36
sysconf	11560
sysfs	84
sysi86	50
time	13
times	43
uadmin	55

Figure 3-29: System Call Numbers (in decimal) (continued)

ulimit	63
umask	60
umount	22
uname	57
unlink	10
ustat	57
utime	30
wait	7
waitpid	7
write	4
reserved	40
reserved	58
reserved	64–78
reserved	105

Some system calls have interfaces that vary slightly from the standard template.

`int brk(char *endds);`
> This system call sets the process break (the end of the data segment) to the value of `endds`. The value of register `%eax` is unspecified for successful returns.

`execve`
> Any return from this system call is an error; thus after the `lcall` instruction, the carry flag is unspecified in the EFLAGS register.

`fork`
> After the `lcall` instruction for a successful call, register `%edx` contains 0 for the parent and non-zero for the child process. In the parent process, register `%eax` holds the child process number; it holds an unspecified value in the child process.

`int getdents(int fd, struct dirent *buf, int count);`
> This call reads directory entries from file descriptor `fd`; `buf` gives the address of the buffer into which the entries are placed, and `count` gives the buffer length in bytes. The return value tells how many bytes were placed into the buffer.

`getegid` and `getgid`
> These calls share an entry into the kernel. After the `lcall` instruction, register `%eax` holds the real group ID; register `%edx` holds the effective group ID.

`geteuid` and `getuid`
> These calls share an entry into the kernel. After the `lcall` instruction, register `%eax` holds the real user ID; register `%edx` holds the effective user ID.

`getpgrp`, `setpgrp`, `setsid`, and `setpgid`
> These calls share an entry into the kernel. A hidden argument (that is, one pushed onto the stack after the return address to the caller of the system library function, followed by another word which is a place holder for the normal return address) determines the service requested: 0 for `getpgrp`, 1 for `setpgrp`, 2 for `setpgid`, 3 for `setsid`, 4 is *reserved*, and 5 is *reserved*.

`getpid` and `getppid`
> These calls share an entry into the kernel. After the `lcall` instruction, register `%eax` holds the process ID; register `%edx` holds the parent process ID.

`msgctl`, `msgget`, `msgrcv`, and `msgsnd`
> These calls share an entry into the kernel. A hidden initial argument (that is, one pushed onto the stack before the return address to the caller of the system library function, followed by the normal return address) determines the service requested: 0 for `msgget`, 1 for `msgctl`, 2 for `msgrcv`, and 3 for `msgsnd`. The function's other arguments occupy correspondingly higher positions in the stack.

`pipe`
> After the `lcall` instruction for a successful call, register `%eax` holds the file descriptor open for reading; register `%edx` holds the file descriptor open for writing.

`semctl`, `semget`, and `semop`
> These calls share an entry into the kernel. A hidden initial argument (that is, one pushed onto the stack before the return address to the caller of the system library function, followed by the normal return address) determines the service requested: 0 for `semctl`, 1 for `semget`, and 2 for `semop`. The function's other arguments occupy correspondingly higher positions in the stack.

`shmat, shmctl, shmdt,` and `shmget`
>These calls share an entry into the kernel. A hidden initial argument (that is, one pushed onto the stack before the return address to the caller of the system library function, followed by the normal return address) determines the service requested: 0 for `shmat`, 1 for `shmctl`, 2 for `shmdt`, and 3 for `shmget`. The function's other arguments occupy correspondingly higher positions in the stack.

`sighold, sigignore, signal, sigpause, sigrelse,` and `sigset`
>These calls share an entry into the kernel. The first argument to each is a signal number, which the kernel checks for flag bits to determine the requested service: 0 for `signal`, 0x100 for `sigset`, 0x200 for `sighold`, 0x400 for `sigrelse`, 0x800 for `sigignore` and 0x1000 for `sigpause`. For the `signal` and `sigset` entries, a hidden argument placed in the `%edx` register points to the user level function that is to receive control if the user signal handler exits via a return. After the `lcall` instruction for a successful call, register `%eax` has the proper return value.

`sync`
>This function has no defined return value. The value of register `%eax` is unspecified after the `lcall` instruction.

`int sysi86(int cmd, int *fp_kind);`
>When `cmd` has the value 40, this call determines whether the machine has an Intel387 coprocessor or if the emulator is being used. It sets the word to which `fp_kind` points as follows: If bit 2 is on, there is either an Intel287™ or Intel387 coprocessor present; if bit 1 is also on, then it is an Intel387 coprocessor, otherwise it is an Intel287 coprocessor. If bit 2 is not on but bit 1 is on, then the Intel387 emulator is being used. If neither of the two bits is on, then there is no support for floating-point instructions.

`int uname(struct utsname *name);`
>This call and `ustat` share an entry into the kernel. Before the `lcall` instruction 4(`%esp`) contains `name`, 8(`%esp`) contains an unspecified value, and 12(`%esp`) contains the value 0.

`int ustat(int dev, struct ustat *buf);`
>This call and `uname` share an entry into the kernel. Before the `lcall` instruction, 4(`%esp`) contains `buf`, 8(`%esp`) contains `dev`, and 12(`%esp`) contains the value 2.

```
pid_t waitpid(pid_t pid, int *stat_loc, int options);
```
This call and `wait` share an entry into the kernel. Before the `lcall` instruction, if the `ZF`, `PF`, `SF` and `OF` flag bits are all set simultaneously in the EFLAGS register, then this is interpreted as a `waitpid` call; otherwise it is interpreted as a `wait` call.

Future Directions

A future version of the system will hide the low-level interface between application programs and the operating system. Instead of executing the `lcall` instructions directly, applications will go through a level of indirection to access system services.

Exception Interface

As the Intel386 architecture manuals describe, the processor changes mode to handle *exceptions*, which may be synchronous, floating-point/coprocessor, or asynchronous. Synchronous and floating-point/coprocessor exceptions, being caused by instruction execution, can be explicitly generated by a process. This section, therefore, specifies those exception types with defined behavior. The Intel386 architecture classifies exceptions as *faults*, *traps*, and *aborts*. See the Intel *80386 Programmer's Reference Manual* for more information about their differences.

Hardware Exception Types

The operating system defines the following correspondence between hardware exceptions and the signals specified by `signal(BA_OS)`.

Figure 3-30: Hardware Exceptions and Signals

Number	Exception Name	Signal
0	divide error fault	SIGFPE
1	single step trap/fault	SIGTRAP
2	nonmaskable interrupt	none
3	breakpoint trap	SIGTRAP
4	overflow trap	SIGSEGV
5	bounds check fault	SIGSEGV
6	invalid opcode fault	SIGILL
7	no coprocessor fault	SIGFPE
8	double fault abort	none
9	coprocessor overrun abort	SIGSEGV
10	invalid TSS fault	none
11	segment not present fault	none
12	stack exception fault	SIGSEGV
13	general protection fault/abort	SIGSEGV
14	page fault	SIGSEGV
15	(reserved)	
16	coprocessor error fault	SIGFPE
17	alignment check (i486 processor only)	SIGBUS
other	(unspecified)	SIGILL

Several trap types can generate either a signal or none. For the "stack exception" and "page fault" traps, if the access is to a virtual address that should be accessible to the process, then the normal actions take place and no signals are generated. Otherwise the SIGSEGV signal is generated as expected.

Floating-point instructions exist in the architecture, but they may be implemented either in hardware (via the Intel387 coprocessor) or in software (via the Intel387 emulator). In the case of "no coprocessor" exception, if the Intel387 emulator is configured into the kernel, the process receives no signal. Instead, the system intercepts the exception, emulates the instruction, and returns control to the process. A process receives SIGFPE for the "no coprocessor" exception only when the indicated floating-point instruction is illegal (invalid operands, etc.).

Software Trap Types

Because the `int` instruction generates traps, some hardware exceptions can be generated by software. However, the `int` instruction generates only traps and not faults; so it is not possible to match the exact hardware generated faults in software.

Signal Stack

This section on signal stack details is at Level 2.

In order for a process to handle signals sent to it by the system, it must first register the signal handler with the system. The mechanism for doing so is the `signal` system call. However, in addition to the normal arguments for the `signal` system call, the `signal` library routine in **libc** places the address of a special routine (for illustration, the routine is labeled `_sigreturn`) that receives control when the user signal handler exits via a return statement in register `%edx`. Figure 3-31 is an example `signal` library routine which is functionally equivalent to the one in the system libraries.

Figure 3-31: Example `signal` **Library Routine**

```
        .globl signal
        .globl errno
signal:
        movl    $SIGNAL,%eax
        movl    $_sigreturn,%edx
        lcall   $0x7,$0
        jc      signal_error
        xorl    %eax,%eax
        ret
signal_error:
        movl    %eax,errno
        movl    $-1,%eax
        ret
```

When a signal is delivered to a process, the system builds a data structure on
the stack and passes control to the user signal handler. The information placed
on the stack makes it appear as if the user signal handler has been called from
the _sigreturn routine which was previously registered with the system. The
user signal handler may terminate by executing a return statement, by calling
the longjmp function, or by terminating the process.

If the user signal handler returns control to the _sigreturn routine, then the
routine will return control to the system to restore the environment of the interrupted process and continue execution of that process at the point of interruption. The _sigreturn routine returns control to the system via a call gate that
is different from that of the normal system call interface. An example of the
_sigreturn routine is shown in Figure 3-32.

Figure 3-32: Returning from Signal Handler

```
_sigreturn:
        addl    $4,%esp
        lcall   $0xf,$0
```

The data structure built on the stack upon entry to the user signal handler contains the signal number, the contents of the user registers, and the floating-point
state and registers. These appear as arguments to the user signal handler. Figure 3-33 shows the stack content upon entry to the user signal handler (refer to
the `struct _fpstackframe` description in the header files `<ieeefp.h>` and
`<sys/reg.h>` in the "System Data Interface" section for a description of the
stack frame format).

Figure 3-33: Signal State Structure

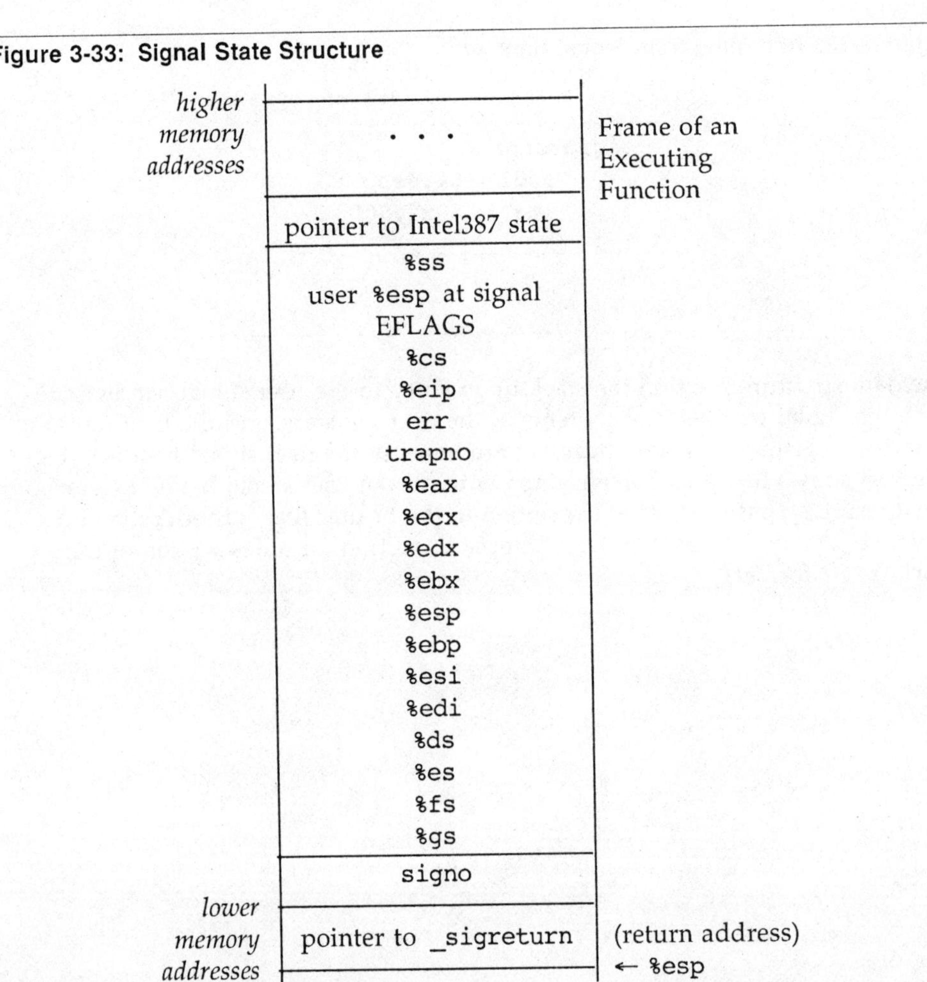

The contents of the %eip register placed on the stack depend on whether the signal was generated as a result of a *trap* or a *fault*, consult the Intel *80386 Programmer's Reference Manual* for more information.

The Intel387 coprocessor state structure is declared in Figure 3-34.

Figure 3-34: Intel387 Coprocessor State Structure

```
struct _fpreg {
        unsigned short significand[4];
        unsigned short exponent;
};

struct _fpstate {
        unsigned long cw,
                      sw,
                      tag,
                      ipoff,
                      cssel,
                      dataoff,
                      datasel;
        struct _fpreg _st[8];
        unsigned long status;
};
```

When the signal is caused by a floating-point exception, then the Intel387 coprocessor is reinitialized upon entry to the user signal handler. The signal handler can safely use the floating-point unit without disturbing the state of the process which was interrupted. However, because of the reinitialization, the contents of the status word (sw) is not reliable, the status of the Intel387 coprocessor at the time of the exception is contained in the status field of the Intel387 coprocessor state structure.

Applications always must store stack information above the stack pointer, because signals can arrive asynchronously. If an application places data below the current stack pointer, a signal's arrival could overwrite the original data, leading to undefined behavior. Programs that violate the stack conventions in this way do not conform to the iBCS.

Future Directions

A future version of the system will hide the low-level interface between application programs and the operating system. When a process receives a signal, the detailed stack manipulation will be transparent to the application.

Process Initialization

This section describes the machine state that exec(BA_OS) creates for "infant" processes, including argument passing, register usage, stack frame layout, etc. Programming language systems use this initial program state to establish a standard environment for their application programs. As an example, a C program begins executing at a function named main, conventionally declared in the way shown in Figure 3-35.

Figure 3-35: Declaration for main

```
extern int main(int argc, char *argv[], char *envp[]);
```

Briefly, argc is a non-negative argument count; argv is an array of argument strings, with argv[argc]==0; and envp is an array of environment strings, also terminated by a null pointer.

Although this section does not describe C program initialization, it gives the information necessary to implement the call to main or to the entry point for a program in any other language.

Special Registers

As the Intel386 architecture defines, several state registers control and monitor the processor: the Machine Status Word register (MSW, also known as register %cr0), EFLAGS register, the floating-point status register, and the floating-point control register. Application programs cannot access the full EFLAGS register directly; because they run in the processor's *user mode*, and the instructions to write some of the bits of the EFLAGS register are privileged. Nonetheless, a program has access to many of the flags in the EFLAGS register. Flags identified with an "*" below are not modifiable by a user mode process; they either have unspecified values or do not affect user program behavior. At process initialization, the EFLAGS register contains the values shown in Figure 3-36.

Figure 3-36: EFLAGS Register Fields

Flag	Value	Note
CF	unspecified	Carry flag
PF	unspecified	Parity flag
AF	unspecified	Auxiliary carry flag
ZF	unspecified	Zero flag
SF	unspecified	Sign flag
TF	unspecified	Trap flag
IF*	unspecified	Interrupt enable
DF	0	Direction flag, low to high direction
OF	unspecified	Overflow flag
IOPL*	unspecified	I/O privilege level
NT*	unspecified	Nested task
RF*	unspecified	Resume flag
VM*	unspecified	Virtual 8086 mode
AC	unspecified	Alignment check (i486 processor only)

The Intel386 architecture defines floating-point instructions, and those instructions work whether the processor has a hardware floating-point unit or not. (A system may provide hardware or software floating-point facilities.) Consequently, the contents of the MSW register is not specified, letting the system set it according to the hardware configuration. In any case, however, the processor presents a working floating-point implementation, including the Intel387 coprocessor status and control word registers with the following values at process initialization.

Figure 3-37: Floating-Point Control Word

Field	Value	Note
IC	1	Affine infinity (for compatibility)
RC	00	Round to nearest or even
PC	10	53-bit (double precision)
PM	1	Precision masked
UM	1	Underflow masked
OM	0	Overflow
ZM	0	Zero divide
DM	1	Denormalized operand masked
IM	0	Invalid operation

Although the special registers are accessible to the user program, if any of the pre-initialized fields in these special registers are modified by the user program, the program does not conform to the iBCS and the behavior of the program is undefined.

Process Stack and Registers

When a process receives control, its stack holds the arguments and environment from exec(BA_OS).

Figure 3-38: Initial Process Stack

	Unspecified	*High addresses*
	Information block, including argument strings, environment strings . . . (size varies)	
	Unspecified	
	0 word	
	Environment pointers . . . (one word each)	
	0 word	
4(%esp)	Argument pointers . . . (*Argument count* words)	
0(%esp)	Argument count	
	Undefined	*Low addresses*

Argument strings and environment strings appear in no specific order within the information block; the system makes no guarantees about their arrangement. The system also may leave an unspecified amount of memory between the null auxiliary vector entry and the beginning of the information block.

General and floating-point register values are unspecified at process entry, with the exceptions appearing below. Consequently, a program that requires registers to have specific values must set them explicitly during process initialization. It must *not* rely on the operating system to set all registers to 0.

`%ebp` The content of this register is undefined at process initialization time, but the user code must mark the deepest stack frame by setting the frame pointer to zero. No other frame's `%ebp` can have a zero value.

`%esp`   Performing its usual job, the stack pointer holds the address of the
bottom of the stack, which is guaranteed to be word aligned.

`%cs`, `%ds`, `%es`, `%ss`
The segment registers are initialized so that the user process can
address the code, data, and stack segments using a 32-bit virtual
address. Although a program may alter the contents of these registers to point to other physical memory segments allocated by the system, such actions must be done very carefully or it may lead to
undefined behavior.

Every process has a stack, but the system defines *no* fixed stack address. Furth-
ermore, a program's stack address can change from one system to another —
even from one process invocation to another. Thus the process initialization
code must use the stack address in `%esp`. Data in the stack segment at
addresses below the stack pointer contain undefined values.

The `%esp` register must point to an address within the stack segment at all
times. If the `%esp` register is changed to point outside of the stack (such as to a
static data object or an address allocated dynamically in the heap), then the
behavior of the program is undefined.

The argument and environment vectors transmit information from one application program to another. Null pointers terminate both vectors.

In the following example, the stack resides below `0x7fffffff`, growing toward
lower addresses. The process receives three arguments:

- cp

- src

- dst

It also inherits two environment strings (this example is not intended to show a
fully configured execution environment).

- HOME=/home/386BCS

- PATH=/home/386BCS/bin:/usr/bin:

The initialization sequence preserves the stack pointer's word alignment. Figure 3-39 shows an example of the initial contents of the process stack.

Figure 3-39: Example Process Stack

	\0	*pad*	*pad*	*pad*	*High addresses*
	b	i	n	:	
	u	s	r	/	
0x7ffffff0	i	n	:	/	
	c	s	/	b	
	3	8	6	B	
	o	m	e	/	
0x7fffffe0	H	=	/	h	
	\0	P	A	T	
	6	B	C	S	
	e	/	3	8	
0x7fffffd0	/	h	o	m	
	O	M	E	=	
	s	t	\0	H	
	r	c	\0	d	
0x7fffffc0	c	p	\0	s	
	0				
	0x7fffffdd				
	0x7fffffcb				*Environment vector*
0x7fffffb0	0				
	0x7fffffc7				
	0x7fffffc3				
	0x7fffffc0				*Argument vector*
0(%esp), 0x7fffffa0	3				*Argument count*
	Undefined				*Low addresses*

Coding Examples

This section discusses example code sequences for fundamental operations such as calling functions, accessing static objects, and transferring control from one part of a program to another. Previous sections discuss how a program may use the machine or the operating system, and they specify what a program may and may not assume about the execution environment. Unlike previous material, the information here illustrates how operations *may* be done following the conventions, not how they *must* be done.

As before, examples use the ANSI C language. Other programming languages may use the same conventions displayed below, but failure to do so does *not* prevent a program from conforming to the iBCS.

Examples below show code fragments with various simplifications. They are intended to explain addressing modes, not to show optimal code sequences nor to reproduce compiler output.

Data Objects

In the Intel386 architecture, all memory reference instructions can address any location within the 32-bit address space, because the instructions can hold a 32-bit address directly. References to statically allocated objects can be done directly using their 32-bit addresses.

Figure 3-40: Global Data Access Example

<table>
<tr><td>C</td><td>Assembly</td></tr>
</table>

```
extern int src;                      globl    src, dst, ptr
extern int dst;
extern int *ptr;
static int inc = 123;        inc:    .long    123
ptr = &dst;                          movl     $dst,ptr
*ptr = src + inc;                    movl     ptr,%eax
                                     movl     src,%edx
                                     addl     inc,%edx
                                     movl     %edx,(%eax)
```

Stack-based objects (such as arguments or function local variables) can be
addressed with offsets from either the stack frame pointer register or the stack
pointer register, depending on whether the frame pointer is set up or not. The
32-bit address of a stack-based object can be calculated easily using the lea
instruction of the Intel386 architecture.

Figure 3-41: Local Data Access Example

C	Assembly

```
foo(src) int src;                    .globl   foo, inc
{                            foo:    pushl    %ebp
    int dst;                         movl     %esp,%ebp
    int *ptr;                        subl     $8,%esp
    extern int inc;
    ptr = &dst;                      leal     -4(%ebp),%eax
                                     movl     %eax,-8(%ebp)
    *ptr = src + inc;                movl     -8(%ebp),%eax
                                     movl     8(%ebp),%edx
                                     addl     inc,%edx
                                     movl     %edx,(%eax)
                                     movl     %ebp,%esp
}                                    popl     %esp
                                     ret
```

Function Calls

Programs use the `call` instruction to make direct function calls. A `call` instruction's destination is relative to the value of the program counter, and can reach any address in the 32-bit virtual space.

Figure 3-42: Function Call Example

C	Assembly

```
extern void function();          .globl   function
function();                      call     function
```

Indirect function calls use the indirect `call` instruction.

Figure 3-43: Indirect Function Call Example

C	Assembly
| ```
extern void (*ptr)();
extern void name();
register void (*p)();
ptr = name;
(*ptr)();
p = name;
(*p)();
``` | ```
.globl   ptr, name


movl     $name,ptr
call     *ptr
movl     $name,%edi
call     *%edi
``` |

Parameter Passing

All parameters are passed via the stack. The space for on-stack arguments is allocated on a per-call basis by the calling function. And if the function returns an aggregate object, then the pointer to the caller-allocated space is pushed last onto the stack.

Figure 3-44: Parameter Passing Example

<table>
<tr><td align="center">C</td><td align="center">Assembly</td></tr>
</table>

```
struct s_t {int i1;
    double d1;} s1, s2;
struct s_t func() {




    return s2;










}
s1 = func();
```

```
func:   popl    %eax
        xchgl   %eax,0(%esp)
        pushl   %ebp
        movl    %esp,%ebp
        pushl   %eax
        movl    %eax,-4(%ebp)
        movl    $s2,%edx
        movl    (%edx),%ecx
        movl    %ecx,(%eax)
        movl    4(%edx),%ecx
        movl    %ecx,4(%eax)
        movl    8(%edx),%ecx
        movl    %ecx,8(%eax)
        movl    %ebp,%esp
        popl    %esp
        ret

        subl    $12,%esp
        pushl   %esp
        call    func
        movl    $s1,%edx
        movl    (%eax),%ecx
        movl    %ecx,(%edx)
        movl    4(%eax),%ecx
        movl    %ecx,4(%edx)
        movl    8(%eax),%ecx
        movl    %ecx,8(%edx)
```

Branching

Programs use branch instructions to control their execution flow. As defined by the Intel386 architecture, branch instructions hold an EIP-relative value with a signed 32-bit range, allowing a jump to any location within the virtual address space.

Figure 3-45: Branch Instruction

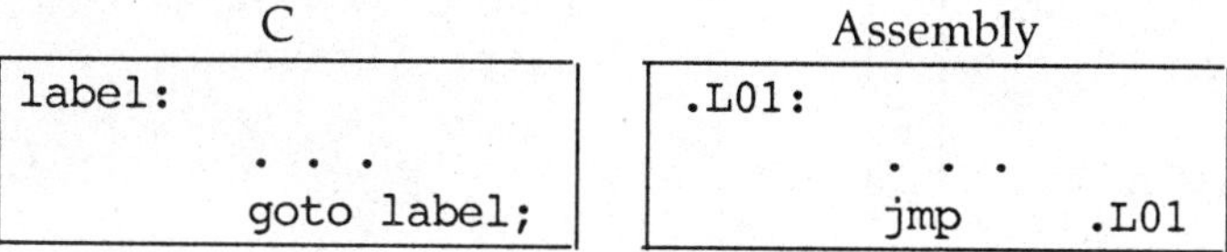

C switch statements provide multiway selection. When the case labels of a switch statement satisfy grouping constraints, the compiler may implement the selection with an address table. The following examples use several simplifying conventions to hide irrelevant details:

- The selection expression resides in register %eax;

- case label constants begin at zero;

- case labels, default, and the address table use assembly names .Lcase*i*, .Ldef, and .Ltab, respectively.

Address table entries for absolute code contain virtual addresses; the selection code extracts an entry's value and jumps to that address.

Figure 3-46: `switch` **Code**

<table>
<tr><th>C</th><th>Assembly</th></tr>
<tr><td>

```
switch (j)
{
case 0:
    . . .
case 2:
    . . .
case 3:
    . . .
default:
    . . .
}
```

</td><td>

```
            cmpl    $3, %eax
            ja      .Ldef
            jmp     *.Ltab(,%eax,4)
.Ltab:      .long   .Lcase0
            .long   .Ldef
            .long   .Lcase2
            .long   .Lcase3
```

</td></tr>
</table>

C Stack Frame

Figure 3-47 shows the C stack frame organization. It conforms to the standard stack frame with designated roles for unspecified areas in the standard frame.

Figure 3-47: C Stack Frame

Base	Offset	Contents	
%ebp	$4n+8$	argument word n	*High addresses*
		. . .	
	8	argument word 0	
	4	return address	
%ebp	0	caller's %ebp	
%ebp	-4	x words local space: automatic variables, temporaries,	
%ebp	$-4x$	etc.	
%esp	12		
%esp	8	caller's %edi	
	4	caller's %esi	
%esp	0	caller's %ebx	*Low addresses*

A C stack frame doesn't normally change size during execution. The exception is dynamically allocated stack memory, discussed below. By convention, a function allocates automatic (local) variables in the middle of its frame and references them as negative offsets from %ebp. Its incoming arguments reside in the previous frame, referenced as positive offsets from %ebp. If necessary, a function may save the values of %edi, %esi, and %ebx in the positions shown and restores their values before returning to the caller. The positions of the saved registers may differ from the diagram above, depending on which of these three registers the function saves and restores. The compiler may also choose to save these registers in a different area within the stack frame.

Variable Argument List

Previous sections describe the rules for passing arguments. Unfortunately, some otherwise portable C programs depend on the argument passing scheme, implicitly assuming that 1) all arguments reside on the stack, and 2) arguments appear in increasing order on the stack. Programs that make these assumptions never have been portable, but they have worked on many machines, including the Intel386. Nonetheless, portable C programs should use the facilities defined in the header files <stdarg.h> or <varargs.h> to deal with variable argument lists.

There is no change to the code generated by a compiler when a function uses the <varargs.h> or the ANSI C language ellipses facilities. The standard argument passing and function calling conventions allow for the direct access to the arguments on the stack in the same order as they are passed.

Figure 3-48: Argument Passing with <varargs.h>

Call	Argument	Stack address
h(1.414,	word 0, 1.414	8(%ebp)
	word 1, 1.414	
1,	1	16(%ebp)
2.998e10,	word 0, 2.998e10	20(%ebp)
	word 1, 2.998e10	
'x',	'x'	28(%ebp)
2.718);	word 0, 2.718	32(%ebp)
	word 1, 2.718	

NOTE Although the Intel386 architecture does not require doubleword alignment for double-precision values, for data structure compatibility with other Intel architectures, it is recommended that double-precision values be doubleword aligned.

The actual implementation of <varargs.h> or of the ANSI prototype mechanism is left to the individual compilers; the implementation does not affect iBCS conformance.

Allocating Stack Space Dynamically

Unlike some other languages, C does not need dynamic stack allocation *within* a stack frame. Frames are allocated dynamically on the program stack, depending on program execution, but individual stack frames can have static sizes. Nonetheless, the architecture supports dynamic allocation for those languages that require it, and the standard calling sequence and stack frame support it as well. Thus languages that need dynamic stack frame sizes can call C functions, and vice versa.

Figure 3-47 shows the layout of the C stack frame. The double line divides the area referenced from %ebp from the area referenced from %esp. Dynamic space is allocated below the line, as a downward growing heap whose size changes as required. Typical C functions have no space in the heap. All areas above the heap in the current frame have a known size to the compiler. Dynamic stack allocation thus takes the following steps.

1. Stack frames are word aligned; dynamic allocation must preserve this property. Thus the function rounds (up) the desired byte count to a multiple of 4.

2. The function decreases the stack pointer by the rounded byte count, increasing its frame size. At this point, the "new" space resides just below the register save area at the bottom of the stack.

3. The function copies the register save area (three or fewer words) to the bottom of the stack, effectively moving the new space up into the frame.

> **NOTE** Whether a compiler chooses to save the caller's register variables in the manner shown in Figure 3-47 is irrelevant to the dynamic stack allocation implementation. Some compilers will save their registers in this %esp-relative manner and therefore a proper implementation of an external dynamic stack allocation function must relocate this area of three words for its caller. If the dynamic stack allocation function is implemented as an external function, it does not know whether the register save area was actually used by its caller or not, it therefore cannot use the three words as part of the newly allocated space. If the implementation of dynamic stack allocation is done inline by the compiler, then the compiler has total control of the stack frame and therefore will not need to concern itself with where the registers are saved.

Even in the presence of signals, dynamic allocation is "safe." If a signal interrupts allocation, one of three things can happen.

- The signal handler can return. The process then resumes the dynamic allocation from the point of interruption.

- The signal handler can execute a non-local goto, or `longjmp` [see `setjmp`(BA_LIB)]. This resets the process to a new context in a previous stack frame, automatically discarding the dynamic allocation.

- The process can terminate.

Regardless of when the signal arrives during dynamic allocation, the result is a consistent (though possibly dead) process.

To illustrate, assume a program wants to allocate 50 bytes, and it has saved three registers in the bottom of the frame. The first step is rounding 50 to 52, making it a multiple of 4. Figure 3-49 shows how the stack frame changes.

Figure 3-49: Dynamic Stack Allocation

	Original	Intermediate	Final	
`0(%ebp)`	arguments and automatic variables	arguments and automatic variables	arguments and automatic variables	`0(%ebp)`
`12(%esp)`	save area 3 words	save area 3 words	old save area 3 words	
`0(%esp)`				
	undefined	+++++++++ new space 52 bytes +++++++++	+++++++++ new space 52 bytes +++++++++	
		undefined	save area 3 words	`12(%esp)` `0(%esp)`

New space starts at `12(%esp)`. As described, every dynamic allocation in *this* function will return a new area starting at `12(%esp)`, leaving previous heap objects untouched (other functions could have different heap addresses). Consequently, the compiler should compute the absolute address for each area, avoiding relative references. Otherwise, future allocations in the same frame would destroy the heap's integrity.

Existing stack objects reside at fixed offsets from the frame pointer (`%ebp`). Dynamic allocation preserves those offsets, because the frame pointer does not change and the objects relative to it do not move. Objects relative to the stack pointer (`%esp`) move, but their `%esp`-*relative* positions do not change. Accordingly, compilers arrange not to publicize the absolute address of any object in the bottom half of the stack frame (in a way that violates the scope rules). `%esp`-relative references stay valid after dynamic allocation, but absolute addresses do not.

No special code is needed to free dynamically allocated stack memory. The function return resets the stack pointer and removes the entire stack frame, including the heap, from the stack. Naturally, a program should not reference heap objects after they have gone out of scope.

Allocating Heap Space Dynamically

Due to the data alignment requirements of the Intel386 architecture, all dynamic heap memory allocation facilities such as `malloc`(BA_OS) must return blocks of memory aligned on a 0 mod 4 boundary.

Identifying the Processor

It may be necessary for some applications to identify whether the enhanced features of the Intel486 processor are available at run time. To do so, the code sequence shown in Figure 3-50 should be used. The code sequence will return a zero value (0) if the processor is an Intel386 processor, it will return a non-zero value otherwise.

Application programs should not depend on this identification sequence if the programs can be executed on a heterogeneous multiprocessor system with both Intel386 processors and Intel486 processors, where user processes may be assigned to different processors dynamically during execution.

Figure 3-50: Processor Identification

```
test_i386: / %esp register must be aligned on 0 mod 4 address
       pushf                     / save EFLAGS register
       mov    0(%esp),%eax / get value of EFLAGS
       xor    $0x40000,%eax/ flip AC bit in EFLAGS
       push   %eax
       popf                      / load new EFLAGS
       pushf                     / save new EFLAGS
       pop    %eax
       xor    0(%esp),%eax / see if AC bit is changed
       and    $0x40000,%eax/ %eax is zero if i386 CPU
       popf                      / restore original EFLAGS
       ret
```

OBJECT FILES

Introduction   4-1
Future Directions   4-1

COFF File Format   4-2
COFF File Header   4-2
COFF System Header   4-5
COFF Sections   4-7

x.out File Format   4-12
x.out Header   4-13
x.out Extended Header   4-16
x.out Segment Table   4-19
x.out Iteration Record   4-23

Introduction

This chapter describes the object file formats. There are three main types of object files.

- A *relocatable file* holds code and data suitable for linking with other object files to create an executable or a shared object file.

- An *executable file* holds a program suitable for execution; the file specifies how exec(BA_OS) creates a program's process image.

- A *shared library file* holds code and data that contribute to a process image, without being contained in the executable file for the process.

Created by the assembler and link editor, object files are binary representations of programs intended to execute directly on a processor. Programs that require other abstract machines, such as shell scripts, are excluded.

After the introductory material, this chapter focuses on the COFF and x.out file formats and how it pertains to building programs. Chapter 5 also describes parts of the object file, concentrating on the information necessary to execute a program.

Future Directions

A future version of the system will define a new enhanced object file format. The file format will support multiple processors and dynamic linking, while keeping common definitions for the structural information. That new object file format will not be based on COFF. The COFF file format referred to in this specification will not be revised or enhanced beyond its current definition.

This iBCS specifies only the information necessary for executable and shared library files. When the new object file is introduced, the scope of the iBCS will be expanded to include relocatable files as well.

COFF File Format

Figure 4-1 shows a COFF object file's organization.

Figure 4-1: COFF Object File Format

File header
System header
Section header table
Section 1
Section 2
. . .
Unspecified

Headers at the beginning of the file must appear in the order shown in Figure 4-1, and they must be adjacent. Thus, the file header appears at the beginning of the file, followed immediately by the system header, and then the section header table.

Sections hold the bulk of object file information: instructions, data, and so on. Chapter 5 discusses how the system converts a file's sections into a process image's *segments*. The file format defines no fixed positions for sections. Although the figure shows the sections in order, actual files may differ. As shown in Figure 4-1, an object file may have areas whose contents are unspecified. The presence of this extra information does not affect iBCS conformance.

COFF File Header

A file header resides at the beginning and holds a "road map" describing the file's organization. Figure 4-2 shows the file header structure.

Figure 4-2: File Header

```
struct filehdr {
        unsigned short          f_magic;
        unsigned short          f_nscns;
        long                    f_timdat;
        long                    f_symptr;
        long                    f_nsyms;
        unsigned short          f_opthdr;
        unsigned short          f_flags;
};
```

The fields in Figure 4-2 are:

f_magic
: This member's value identifies the processor on which the file must execute. For the Intel386 processor, the value is 0514 (octal) 0x14c (hex).

f_nscns
: This member's value gives the number of entries in the section header table.

f_timdat
: The system ignores this member during process execution. Its value is unspecified.

f_symptr
: The system ignores this member during process execution. Its value is unspecified.

f_nsyms
: The system ignores this member during process execution. Its value is unspecified.

f_opthdr
: This member's value gives the size of the system header. For executable and shared library files, the value must be at least as big as the aouthdr structure, defined below.

f_flags
: This member's value holds various bit flags, describing the file or the machine upon which the file must execute. Flags not defined may also be set in the value, but their meanings are not specified.

Flag definitions for the `f_flags` member appear in Figure 4-3.

Figure 4-3: File Header Flags, `f_flags`

Name	Value (octal)
F_RELFLG	0000001
F_EXEC	0000002
F_LNNO	0000004
F_LSYMS	0000010
F_SWABD	0000100
F_AR16WR	0000200
F_AR32WR	0000400

When set, the flags in Figure 4-3 mean:

F_RELFLG   Relocation information has been stripped from the file.

F_EXEC   The file may be loaded and executed (there are no unresolved external references). Executable and shared library files must have this bit set.

F_LNNO   Line numbers have been stripped from the file.

F_LSYMS   Local symbols have been stripped from the file.

F_SWABD   Bytes in names have been swabbed.

F_AR16WR   Word is 16 bits, byte-reversed.

F_AR32WR   Word is 32 bits, byte-reversed.

COFF System Header

A system header gives information for process creation. Figure 4-4 shows the system header structure.

Figure 4-4: System Header

```
struct aouthdr {
        short  magic;
        short  vstamp;
        long   tsize;
        long   dsize;
        long   bsize;
        long   entry;
        long   tstart;
        long   dstart;
};
```

The fields in Figure 4-4 are:

magic
: This member's value identifies the file type. Figure 4-5 shows the valid types.

vstamp
: The system ignores this member during process execution. Its value is unspecified.

tsize
: The system ignores this member during process execution. Its value is unspecified.

dsize
: The system ignores this member during process execution. Its value is unspecified.

bsize
: The system ignores this member during process execution. Its value is unspecified.

entry
: This member's value gives the entry point for executable files. That is, when the system starts the program associated with an executable file, the first instruction resides at the address in the entry member.

tstart
: The system ignores this member during process execution. Its value is unspecified.

dstart
: The system ignores this member during process execution. Its value is unspecified.

Magic number definitions for the system header appear in Figure 4-5.

Figure 4-5: Magic Numbers in System Header

Value		Meaning
Octal	Hex	
0407	0x107	Text segment is neither write-protected nor sharable; data segment is contiguous with the text segment.
0410	0x108	Data segment starts at the next segment following the text segment, and the text segment is write-protected.
0413	0x10b	Text and data segments are aligned within the object file so it can be directly paged.
0443	0x123	The object file is a shared library.

COFF Sections

An executable or shared library file's section header table is an array of structures, each describing a part of the object file called a section. Typical sections are initial process segment images or information the system needs to prepare the program for execution. Figure 4-6 shows the section header structure.

Figure 4-6: Section Header

```
struct scnhdr {
        char                    s_name[8];
        long                    s_paddr;
        long                    s_vaddr;
        long                    s_size;
        long                    s_scnptr;
        long                    s_relptr;
        long                    s_lnnoptr;
        unsigned short          s_nreloc;
        unsigned short          s_nlnno;
        long                    s_flags;
};
```

The fields in Figure 4-6 are:

s_name   The system ignores this member during process execution. Its value is unspecified.

s_paddr   On systems for which physical addressing is relevant, this member is reserved for the section's physical address. Because UNIX ignores physical addressing for application programs, this member has unspecified contents for executable files and shared objects.

s_vaddr	This member gives the virtual address at which the first byte of the section resides in memory.
s_size	This member gives the section size, in bytes; it may be zero. A section may have a non-zero size without occupying space in the file, as described under s_scnptr.
s_scnptr	This member gives the offset from the beginning of the file at which the first byte of the section resides. If the value is zero, the section occupies no bytes in the file, regardless of the size recorded in s_size.
s_relptr	The system ignores this member during process execution. Its value is unspecified.
s_lnnoptr	The system ignores this member during process execution. Its value is unspecified.
s_nreloc	The system ignores this member during process execution. Its value is unspecified.
s_nlnno	The system ignores this member during process execution. Its value is unspecified.
s_flags	This member tells what kind of section this array element describes or how to interpret the array element's information. Type values and their meanings appear below.

Some entries describe process segments; others give supplementary information and do not contribute to the process image. Section entries may appear in any order. A section header's s_flags member determines the section type. Figure 4-7 shows the defined type values; other values are reserved for future use.

Figure 4-7: Section Types, `s_flags`

Name	Value
STYP_REG	0x00
STYP_DSECT	0x01
STYP_NOLOAD	0x02
STYP_GROUP	0x04
STYP_PAD	0x08
STYP_COPY	0x10
STYP_TEXT	0x20
STYP_DATA	0x40
STYP_BSS	0x80
STYP_INFO	0x200
STYP_OVER	0x400
STYP_LIB	0x800

The defined type values in Figure 4-7 are:

STYP_REG   Regular section (allocated, relocated, loaded).

STYP_DSECT   Dummy section (not allocated, relocated, not loaded).

STYP_NOLOAD   No-load section (not allocated, relocated, not loaded).

STYP_GROUP   Grouped section (formed from input sections).

STYP_PAD   Padding section (not allocated, not relocated, loaded).

STYP_COPY   Copy section, for a decision function used in updating fields (not allocated, not relocated, loaded; relocation and line-number entries processed normally).

STYP_TEXT   This section type designates an area in the process image for executable instructions and unwritable data. The process image will be created from the section bytes in the file.

STYP_DATA   This section type designates an area in the process image for initialized, writable data. The process image will be created from the section bytes in the file.

STYP_BSS   This section type designates an area in the process image for
                 uninitialized, writable data. Although an object file has a sec-
                 tion header of this type, its s_scnptr will have a zero value,
                 indicating the file has no bytes for the section itself.

STYP_INFO   Comment section (not allocated, not relocated, not loaded).

STYP_OVER   Overlay section (not allocated, relocated, not loaded).

STYP_LIB   This section type designates a section in an executable file that
                 tells what shared libraries the program needs during execution.
                 The format of the section appears below.

When attaching shared libraries during process execution, the system needs the
library path names. The number of shared libraries a process may use is a tunable configuration parameter. This information appears as entries of the form
shown in Figure 4-8.

Figure 4-8: Shared Library Section Entry

```
 __________
|  entsz   |
|__________|
| pathndx  |
|__________|
|   path   |
|  . . .   |
|__________|
```

The fields in Figure 4-8 are:

entsz   This 4-byte word tells how many 4-byte words the entire entry occu-
           pies, including itself.

pathndx   This 4-byte word tells how many 4-byte words appear before the
           path name in the entry, starting from the entsz word.

path   This is the path name itself, null-terminated and padded to a word
           boundary.

To illustrate, a library section with two entries appears in Figure 4-9. The first
entry contains the path name /shlib/libc_s, while the second entry holds
/dir/lib/example.

Figure 4-9: Example Shared Library Section

6			
2			
/	s	h	l
i	b	/	l
i	b	c	_
s	\0	*pad*	*pad*
7			
2			
/	d	i	r
/	l	i	b
/	e	x	a
m	p	l	e
\0	*pad*	*pad*	*pad*

x.out File Format

The x.out object file format described in this section is at Level 2.

This iBCS specifies only the information necessary for executable x.out files. Figure 4-10 shows an x.out object file's organization.

Figure 4-10: x.out Object File Format

Header
Extended header
File segment table
Segment 1
Segment 2
. . .
Unspecified

Headers at the beginning of the file must appear in the order shown in Figure 4-10, and they must be adjacent. Thus, the header appears at the beginning of the file, followed immediately by the extended header, and then the file segment table.

Segments hold the bulk of object file information: instructions, data, and so on. Chapter 5 discusses how the system converts a file's segments into a process image's *segments*. The file format defines no fixed positions for segments. Although the figure shows the segments in order, actual files may differ. As shown in Figure 4-10, an object file may have areas whose contents are unspecified. The presence of this extra information does not affect iBCS conformance.

x.out Header

An x.out header resides at the beginning and holds a "road map" describing the file's organization. Figure 4-11 shows the file header structure.

Figure 4-11: x.out Header

```
struct xexec {
        unsigned short      x_magic;
        unsigned short      x_ext;
        long                x_text;
        long                x_data;
        long                x_bss;
        long                x_syms;
        long                x_reloc;
        long                x_entry;
        char                x_cpu;
        char                x_relsym;
        unsigned short      x_renv;
};
```

The fields in Figure 4-11 are:

x_magic   This member's value identifies the file type. For executable files for the Intel386 processor, the value is `01006` (octal) `0x0206` (hex).

x_ext   This member's value gives the size of the extended header. For executable files, the value must be at least as big as the **xext** structure, defined below.

x_text   The system ignores this member during process execution. Its value is unspecified.

x_data   The system ignores this member during process execution. Its value is unspecified.

x_bss   The system ignores this member during process execution. Its value is unspecified.

x_syms   The system ignores this member during process execution. Its value is unspecified.

x_reloc   The system ignores this member during process execution. Its value is unspecified.

x_entry   This member's value gives the entry point for executable files. That is, when the system starts the program associated with an executable file, the first instruction resides at the address in the x_entry member.

x_cpu   This member's value identifies the processor on which the file must execute. For the Intel386 processor, the value is 0112 (octal) 0x4a (hex).

x_relsym   The system ignores this member during process execution. Its value is unspecified.

x_renv   This member's value holds various bit flags, describing the file or the environment upon which the file must execute. Flags not defined may also be set in the value, but their meanings are not specified.

Flag definitions for the x_renv member appear in Figure 4-12.

Figure 4-12: Header Flags, x_renv

Name	Value
XE_V5	0xc000
XE_SEG	0x0800
XE_ABS	0x0400
XE_ITER	0x0200
XE_VMOD	0x0100
XE_FPH	0x0080
XE_LTEXT	0x0040
XE_LDATA	0x0020
XE_OVER	0x0010
XE_FS	0x0008
XE_PURE	0x0004
XE_SEP	0x0002
XE_EXEC	0x0001

When set, the flags in Figure 4-12 mean:

XE_V5   The file is an x.out file executable on iBCS-conforming systems.

XE_SEG   The file is a segmented x.out file and the segment table is present.

XE_ABS   This flag must be set to zero for iBCS-conforming programs.

XE_ITER   The file contains iterated text and data segments.

XE_VMOD   This flag must be set to zero for iBCS-conforming programs.

XE_FPH   The file requires floating point hardware to execute.

XE_LTEXT   The file requires multiple Intel386 architecture memory segments for the text segments during execution.

XE_LDATA   The file requires multiple Intel386 architecture memory segments for the data segments during execution.

XE_OVER	The file contains text overlays.
XE_FS	The file uses a fixed size stack during execution.
XE_PURE	The file contains pure text segment(s), which are never modified and therefore can be shared among many processes.
XE_SEP	The file uses separate Intel386 architecture instruction and data memory segments during execution.
XE_EXEC	The file is an executable file. This flag must be set to 1 for iBCS-conforming programs.

x.out Extended Header

An extended header gives information for process creation. Figure 4-13 shows the system header structure.

Figure 4-13: System Header

```
struct xext {
        long                    xe_trsize;
        long                    xe_drsize;
        long                    xe_tbase;
        long                    xe_dbase;
        long                    xe_stksize;
        long                    xe_segpos;
        long                    xe_segsize;
        long                    xe_mdtpos;
        long                    xe_mdtsize;
        char                    xe_mdttype;
        char                    xe_pagesize;
        char                    xe_ostype;
        char                    xe_osvers;
        unsigned short          xe_eseg;
        unsigned short          xe_sres;
};
```

The fields in Figure 4-13 are:

xe_trsize   The system ignores this member during process execution. Its
             value is unspecified.

xe_drsize   The system ignores this member during process execution. Its
             value is unspecified.

xe_tbase   The system ignores this member during process execution. Its
             value is unspecified.

xe_dbase   The system ignores this member during process execution. Its
             value is unspecified.

`xe_stksize`	This member gives the stack size used by the program if the XE_FS flag was set in the `x_renv` field of the header. Otherwise this member is ignored and its value is unspecified.
`xe_segpos`	This member gives the offset from the beginning of the file at which the first byte of the segment table resides.
`xe_segsize`	This is the size of the segment table. For executable files, the value must be at least as big as the `xseg` structure, defined below.
`xe_mdtpos`	The system ignores this member during process execution. Its value is unspecified.
`xe_mdtsize`	The system ignores this member during process execution. Its value is unspecified.
`xe_mdttype`	The system ignores this member during process execution. Its value is unspecified.
`xe_pagesize`	The system ignores this member during process execution. Its value is unspecified.
`xe_ostype`	The system ignores this member during process execution. Its value is unspecified.
`xe_osvers`	The system ignores this member during process execution. Its value is unspecified.
`xe_eseg`	The system ignores this member during process execution. Its value is unspecified.
`xe_sres`	The system ignores this member during process execution. Its value is unspecified.

x.out Segment Table

An executable file's segment table is an array of structures, each describing a part of the object file called a segment. Typical segments are initial process segment images or information the system needs to prepare the program for execution. Figure 4-14 shows the segment table structure.

Figure 4-14: Segment Table

```
struct xseg {
        unsigned short      xs_type;
        unsigned short      xs_attr;
        unsigned short      xs_seg;
        char                xs_align;
        char                xs_cres;
        long                xs_filpos;
        long                xs_psize;
        long                xs_vsize;
        long                xs_rbase;
        unsigned short      xs_noff;
        unsigned short      xs_sres;
        long                xs_lres;
};
```

The fields in Figure 4-14 are:

xs_type   This member tells what kind of segment this array element describes or how to interpret the array element's information. Type values and their meanings appear below.

xs_attr   This member's value holds various bit flags, describing the segment contents attributes. Within this iBCS specification, only the flags applying to XS_TTEXT and XS_TDATA segments are described below.

`xs_seg`	This member gives the Intel386 architecture memory segment selector number corresponding to this segment. For iBCS-conforming programs, this value must have the three least significant bits (mask `0x0007`) set, indicating an LDT entry in ring 3 (or user mode) for any `XS_TTEXT` and `XS_TDATA` segments.
`xs_align`	The system ignores this member during process execution. Its value is unspecified.
`xs_cres`	The system ignores this member during process execution. Its value is unspecified.
`xs_filpos`	This member gives the offset from the beginning of the file at which the first byte of the segment resides. If the value is zero, the segment occupies no bytes in the file, regardless of the size recorded in `xs_vsize`.
`xs_psize`	This member gives the segment size, in bytes, within the file. It may be zero.
`xs_vsize`	This member gives the segment size, in bytes, when the program is executing in memory. It may be zero. A segment may have a non-zero size without occupying space in the file, such as uninitialized data segments.
`xs_rbase`	This member gives the relocation base address for the segment.
`xs_noff`	The system ignores this member during process execution. Its value is unspecified.
`xs_sres`	The system ignores this member during process execution. Its value is unspecified.
`xs_lres`	The system ignores this member during process execution. Its value is unspecified.

Some entries describe process segments; others give supplementary information and do not contribute to the process image. Segment entries may appear in any order. A segment table's `xs_type` member determines the segment type. Figure 4-15 shows the defined type values; other values are reserved for future use.

Figure 4-15: Segment Types, `xs_type`

Name	Value
XS_TNULL	0
XS_TTEXT	1
XS_TDATA	2
XS_TSYMS	3
XS_TREL	4
XS_TSESTR	5
XS_TGRPS	6
XS_TIDATA	64
XS_TTSS	65
XS_TLFIX	66
XS_TDNAME	67
XS_TDTEXT	68
XS_TDFIX	69
XS_TOVTAB	70
XS_T71	71
XS_TSYSTR	72

The defined type values in Figure 4-15 are:

`XS_TNULL`   Unused segment (not allocated, not relocated, not loaded).

`XS_TTEXT`   This segment type designates an area in the process image for executable instructions and unwritable data. The process image will be created from the segment bytes in the file.

`XS_TDATA`   This section type designates an area in the process image for initialized or uninitialized, writable data. The process image will be created from the segment bytes in the file, if any.

`XS_TSYMS`   Symbol table segment (not allocated, relocated, not loaded).

`XS_TREL`   Relocation segment (not allocated, not relocated, not loaded).

`XS_TSESTR`   Segment table's string table segment (not allocated, not relocated, not loaded).

`XS_TGRPS`	Group definitions segment (reserved).
`XS_TIDATA`	Iterated data segment (reserved).
`XS_TTSS`	Intel386 architecture TSS segment (reserved).
`XS_TLFIX`	Loader fixup segment (reserved).
`XS_TDNAME`	Descriptor names segment (reserved).
`XS_TDTEXT`	Debug text segment (reserved).
`XS_TDFIX`	Debug relocation segment (reserved).
`XS_TOVTAB`	Overlay table segment (reserved).
`XS_T71`	Reserved segment type (reserved).
`XS_TSYSTR`	Symbol string table segment (reserved).

The segment attributes flags shown in Figure 4-16 are only meaningful for `XS_TTEXT` and `XS_TDATA` segments.

Figure 4-16: Segment Attributes, `xs_attr`

Name	Value
XS_AMEM	0x8000
XS_AITER	0x0001
XS_AHUGE	0x0002
XS_ABSS	0x0004
XS_APURE	0x0008
XS_AEDOWN	0x0010
XS_APRIV	0x0020
XS_A32BIT	0x0040

When set, the flags in Figure 4-16 mean:

`XS_AMEM`	The segment is a memory image, and the value of the `xs_seg` member is an Intel386 architecture selector number to be placed in the corresponding selector register.

XS_AITER	The segment contains iteration records.
XS_AHUGE	This flag is reserved and is not currently used.
XS_ABSS	The segment contains implicit uninitialized data. All the bytes in the memory image not explicitly initialized by the segment image within the executable file will be initialized to zero.
XS_APURE	The segment only contains executable instructions or read-only data, the memory image will not be modified and may be shared among different processes.
XS_EDOWN	The segment is an Intel386 architecture expand down memory segment.
XS_PRIV	This flag is reserved and is not currently used.
XS_A32BIT	The segment contains 32-bit text/data, this flag must be set to 1 for iBCS-conforming programs.

x.out Iteration Record

An iteration record is used to initialize an area of memory with the same byte patterns repeated a number of times. This is especially useful when initializing a large area of memory, where it is not desirable to keep the large memory image in the executable file.

A segment that contains iteration records will have the XS_AITER flag of the xs_attr member of the segment table entry set. Within the segment image in the executable file, an xiter record is followed immediately by the text or data to be replicated. There can be many iteration records within a single segment image, one following another; therefore it is possible for the xiter records to be improperly aligned. Figure 4-17 shows the iteration record structure.

Figure 4-17: Iteration Record

```
struct xiter {
        long            xi_size;
        long            xi_rep;
        long            xi_offset;
};
```

The fields in Figure 4-17 are:

xw_size
: This member gives the size, in bytes, of the text/data that follows the `xiter` record. The specified number of bytes will be replicated within the memory image. This member may have the value zero, in which case, no bytes are modified in the memory image.

xi_rep
: This member gives the number of times the bytes are to be replicated within the memory image.

xi_offset
: This member gives the offset within the segment where the first byte of the replicated text/data will start.

5 PROGRAM LOADING

Program Loading   5-1
Future Directions   5-1
Sections and Segments   5-1
Creating the Process Image   5-2

Program Loading

This chapter describes the object file information and system actions that create running programs.

Executable and shared libraries statically represent programs. To execute such programs, the system uses the files to create dynamic program representations, or process images. As section "Virtual Address Space" in Chapter 3 of the iBCS describes, a process image has segments that hold its text, data, stack, and so on.

Future Directions

A future version of the system will provide dynamic linking. This chapter will be expanded to describe dynamic linking facilities and how they affect program loading when the new enhanced object file format is defined.

Sections and Segments

Although not required by the file format, a program to be loaded by the system must have one section of each of the following types: STYP_TEXT, STYP_DATA, and STYP_BSS. When the system creates loadable segments' memory images, it gives access permissions based on the type. The system may grant more access than requested. In no case, however, will a segment have write permission unless it is specified explicitly. Figure 5-1 shows the allowable permissions.

Figure 5-1: Segment Permissions

Type	Exact	Allowable
STYP_BSS	Read, write	Read, write, execute
STYP_DATA	Read, write	Read, write, execute
STYP_TEXT	Read, execute	Read, execute

Creating the Process Image

As the system creates or augments a process image, it logically copies a file's segment to a virtual memory segment. When — and if — the system physically reads the file depends on the program's execution behavior, system load, etc. A process does not require a physical page unless it references the logical page during execution, and processes commonly leave many pages unreferenced. Therefore, delaying physical reads frequently obviates them, improving system performance. To obtain this efficiency in practice, executable and shared object files must have segment images whose file offsets and virtual addresses are congruent, modulo the page size.

Virtual addresses and file offsets for the Intel386 architecture segments are congruent modulo 4 KB (0x1000) or larger powers of 2. Because 4 KB is the maximum page size, the files will be suitable for paging.

Figure 5-2 shows an example executable file, and Figure 5-3 shows the section header segments for the file shown in Figure 5-2.

Figure 5-2: Executable File Example

File Offset	File	Virtual Address
0	File header	
	System header	
	Section header table	
	Other information	
0x148	Text segment	0x00000148
	. . .	
	0x1c8 bytes	
0x310	Data segment	0x00400310
	. . .	
	0x6fc bytes	
0xa0c	Other information	
	. . .	

Figure 5-3: Section Header Segments Example

Member	Text	Data	Bss
s_name	unspecified	unspecified	unspecified
s_paddr	unspecified	unspecified	unspecified
s_vaddr	0x00000148	0x00400310	unspecified
s_size	0x1c8	0x6fc	0x1024
s_scnptr	0x148	0x310	0
s_relptr	unspecified	unspecified	unspecified
s_lnnoptr	unspecified	unspecified	unspecified
s_nreloc	unspecified	unspecified	unspecified
s_nlnno	unspecified	unspecified	unspecified
s_flags	STYP_TEXT	STYP_DATA	STYP_BSS

As shown in Figure 5-2, although the example's file offsets and virtual addresses are congruent modulo 4 KB for both text and data, up to four file pages hold impure text or data (depending on page size and file system block size).

- The first text page contains the file header, the system header, the section header table, and other information.

- The last text page may hold a copy of the beginning of data.

- The first data page may hold a copy of the end of text.

- The last data page may contain file information not relevant to the running process.

Logically, the system enforces the memory permissions as if each segment were complete and separate; segments' addresses are adjusted to ensure each logical page in the address space has a single set of permissions. In the example in Figure 5-3, the region of the file holding the end of text and the beginning of data will be mapped twice: at one virtual address for text and at a different virtual address for data.

The end of the data segment requires special handling for uninitialized data, corresponding to the STYP_BSS section. Instead of looking at the s_vaddr member of the STYP_BSS section header, the system inspects the section's s_size member and initializes that many bytes to zero, starting at the end of the STYP_DATA section. Thus if a file's last data page includes information not in the logical memory page, the extraneous data must be set to zero, not the unknown contents of the executable file. "Impurities" in the other three pages are not logically part of the process image; whether the system expunges them is undefined. The memory image for this program is shown in Figure 5-4, assuming 4 KB (0x1000) pages.

Figure 5-4: Process Image Segments Example

Virtual Address	Contents	Segment
0x00000000	*Header padding* 0x148 bytes	
0x00000148	Text segment . . . 0x1c8 bytes	Text
0x00000310	*Data padding* 0xcf0 bytes	
0x00400000	*Text padding* 0x310 bytes	
0x00400310	Data segment . . . 0x6fc bytes	Data
0x00400a0c	Uninitialized data 0x1024 zero bytes	
0x00401a30	*Page padding* 0x5d0 zero bytes	

If an executable file has a section of type STYP_LIB, the system reads the associated section during exec(BA_OS) and attaches the specified shared libraries. The system ignores STYP_LIB sections for shared libraries.

6 LIBRARIES

Introduction 6-1
Future Directions 6-1
Shared Library Information 6-1

C and System Services Library 6-3

Network Services Library 6-7

X-Windows Version 11 Release 4 Library 6-10

System Data Interfaces 6-28
Data Definitions 6-28

Introduction

As a *binary* specification, the iBCS provides shared library organization; that is,
it tells what services reside in what shared libraries. Programs use the mechanism described in Chapter 5 to access their services. The iBCS does not duplicate
the descriptions available in the **SVID** and other references that tell what the
facilities do, how to use them, etc. Moreover, the iBCS specifies only those routines contained in the standard shared libraries. Functions that reside directly in
application files do not appear here. For example, mathematical routines, such
as sin(BA_LIB), would be available in a development environment, but an
application's executable file would contain the associated code. Assuming the
functions themselves are iBCS-conforming, their presence does not affect the
conformance of the application.

Future Directions

Shared libraries will become a standard part of the application execution
environment in a future version of the system using the new standard object file
format. The fixed addresses mentioned in this chapter will be replaced by
dynamic linking, making library maintenance easier and reducing the adminis-
trative concerns for library developers.

Shared Library Information

This section on shared libraries details is at Level 2. A future version of
the system will provide dynamic linking, eliminating the fixed path names
and fixed addresses of the current system. Although the shared libraries
implementation details are marked as Level 2, the shared libraries and
the interfaces will continue to exist.

The following shared libraries will be supported and will contain all the services
specified here.

libc
: A C language and system services interface library described in this
chapter.

libnsl
: A transport layer interface library described in this chapter.

The following shared library is optional, and if provided it will contain all the services specified here.

libX11   An X-Windows services interface library described in this chapter.

Shared library text segments start at address 0xa0000000 and continue upward within the process virtual address space. Shared library data segments start at address 0xa0400000 within the process virtual address space.

As Chapter 5 describes, executable files contain the names of required shared libraries.

Figure 6-1: System Library Names

Library	File Name
libc	/shlib/libc_s
libnsl	/shlib/libnsl_s
libX11	/usr/X/lib/libX11_s

C and System Services Library

This section on **libc** implementation is at Level 2.

The C language and system services library, **libc**, contains the following routines, along with their assigned virtual addresses.

Figure 6-2: **libc** Contents

`__Fp_Used`	`0xa0400000`
`__fltused`	`0xa0400094`
`_libc__allocs`	`0xa0400014`
`_libc__bufendtab`	`0xa040002c`
`_libc__cleanup`	`0xa0400034`
`_libc__ctype`	`0xa0400004`
`_libc__iob`	`0xa0400024`
`_libc__lastbuf`	`0xa0400028`
`_libc__sibuf`	`0xa0400018`
`_libc__smbuf`	`0xa0400020`
`_libc__sobuf`	`0xa040001c`
`_libc_end`	`0xa0400030`
`_libc_environ`	`0xa0400038`
`_libc_free`	`0xa0400010`
`_libc_malloc`	`0xa0400008`
`_libc_realloc`	`0xa040000c`
reserved	`0xa0400050`
reserved	`0xa0400058`
reserved	`0xa040005c`
`_bufsync`	`0xa0000005`
`_cerror`	`0xa000000a`
`_cleanup`	`0xa000000f`
`_doprnt`	`0xa0000000`
`_filbuf`	`0xa0000014`
`_findbuf`	`0xa0000019`
`_findiop`	`0xa000001e`
`_flsbuf`	`0xa0000023`
`_wrtchk`	`0xa0000028`
`_xflsbuf`	`0xa000002d`

Figure 6-2: libc **Contents** (continued)

abs	0xa0000032
access	0xa0000037
atof	0xa000003c
atoi	0xa0000041
atol	0xa0000046
brk	0xa000004b
calloc	0xa0000050
cfree	0xa0000055
chdir	0xa000005a
chmod	0xa000005f
close	0xa0000064
creat	0xa0000069
ecvt	0xa000006e
errno	0xa040004c
fclose	0xa0000073
fcntl	0xa0000078
fcvt	0xa000007d
fflush	0xa0000082
fgetc	0xa0000087
fgets	0xa000008c
fopen	0xa0000091
fprintf	0xa0000096
fputc	0xa000009b
fputs	0xa00000a0
fread	0xa00000a5
free	0xa00000aa
freopen	0xa00000af
frexp	0xa00000b4
fseek	0xa00000b9
fstat	0xa00000be
fwrite	0xa00000c3
gcvt	0xa00000c8
getchar	0xa00000cd
getenv	0xa00000d2
getopt	0xa00000d7
getpid	0xa00002e9
gets	0xa00000e1

Figure 6-2: libc **Contents** (continued)

getw	0xa00000e6
ioctl	0xa00000eb
isatty	0xa00000f0
isnand	0xa00000f5
kill	0xa00000fa
ldexp	0xa00000ff
lseek	0xa0000104
malloc	0xa0000109
memccpy	0xa000010e
memchr	0xa0000113
memcmp	0xa0000118
memcpy	0xa000011d
memset	0xa0000122
mktemp	0xa0000127
old_tolower	0xa00001b3
old_toupper	0xa00001b8
open	0xa000012c
optarg	0xa0400048
opterr	0xa040003c
optind	0xa0400040
optopt	0xa0400044
printf	0xa0000131
putchar	0xa0000136
puts	0xa000013b
putw	0xa0000140
read	0xa0000145
realloc	0xa000014a
sbrk	0xa000014f
setbuf	0xa0000154
sighold	0xa0000159
sigignore	0xa000015e
signal	0xa0000163
sigpause	0xa0000168
sigrelse	0xa000016d
sigset	0xa0000172
sprintf	0xa0000177
stat	0xa000017c

Figure 6-2: libc **Contents** (continued)

```
strcat      0xa0000181
strchr      0xa0000186
strcmp      0xa000018b
strcpy      0xa0000190
strlen      0xa0000195
strncat     0xa000019a
strncmp     0xa000019f
strncpy     0xa00001a4
strrchr     0xa00001a9
time        0xa00001ae
ungetc      0xa00001bd
unlink      0xa00001c2
utime       0xa00001c7
write       0xa00001cc
```

The **SVID** gives the interfaces to the services given above.

Refer to "System Data Interfaces" later in this chapter for more information.

Network Services Library

This section on **libnsl** implementation is at Level 2.

The network services library, **libnsl**, contains the following routines, along with
their assigned virtual addresses.

Figure 6-3: **libnsl Contents**

__calloc	0xa14004d4
__close	0xa1400508
__errno	0xa14004d8
__fcntl	0xa14004dc
__free	0xa14004e0
__getmsg	0xa14004f0
__ioctl	0xa14004e4
__memcpy	0xa14004e8
__open	0xa1400504
__perror	0xa14004ec
__putmsg	0xa14004f4
__sigset	0xa14004f8
__strlen	0xa14004fc
__ulimit	0xa140050c
__write	0xa1400500
_alloc_buf	0xa1002a0c
_null_tiptr	0xa1001538
_rcv_conn_con	0xa1001f44
_snd_conn_req	0xa1001ddc
_t_aligned_copy	0xa1000ff4
_t_alloc_bufs	0xa1001314
_t_checkfd	0xa1000fa8
_t_do_ioctl	0xa1001284
_t_is_event	0xa1001084
_t_is_ok	0xa10010dc
_t_max	0xa100102c
_t_putback	0xa1001044
_t_setsize	0xa1001510
_ti_user	0xa1400004

Figure 6-3: libnsl **Contents** (continued)

openfiles	0xa1400510
t_accept	0xa1000000
t_alloc	0xa1000005
t_bind	0xa100000a
t_close	0xa100000f
t_connect	0xa1000014
t_errlist	0xa1400070
t_errno	0xa1400038
t_error	0xa1000019
t_free	0xa100001e
t_getinfo	0xa1000023
t_getstate	0xa1000028
t_listen	0xa100002d
t_look	0xa1000032
t_nerr	0xa140003c
t_open	0xa1000037
t_optmgmt	0xa100003c
t_rcv	0xa1000041
t_rcvconnect	0xa1000046
t_rcvdis	0xa100004b
t_rcvrel	0xa1000050
t_rcvudata	0xa1000055
t_rcvuderr	0xa100005a
t_snd	0xa100005f
t_snddis	0xa1000064
t_sndrel	0xa1000069
t_sndudata	0xa100006e
t_sync	0xa1000073
t_unbind	0xa1000078
tiusr_statetbl	0xa1400514

The **SVID** gives the interfaces to many of the services given above. Other interface descriptions appear below.

__calloc   A program sets this pointer to the address of calloc [refer to malloc(BA_OS)].

__close   A program sets this pointer to the address of close(BA_OS).

__errno   A program sets this pointer to the address of errno(BA_ENV).

__fcntl   A program sets this pointer to the address of fcntl(BA_OS).

__free   A program sets this pointer to the address of free [refer to malloc(BA_OS)].

__getmsg   A program sets this pointer to the address of getmsg(NS_OS).

__ioctl   A program sets this pointer to the address of ioctl(BA_OS).

__memcpy   A program sets this pointer to the address of memcpy [refer to memory(BA_LIB)].

__open   A program sets this pointer to the address of open(BA_OS).

__perror   A program sets this pointer to the address if perror(BA_LIB).

__putmsg   A program sets this pointer to the address of putmsg(NS_OS).

__sigset   A program sets this pointer to the address of sigset(BA_OS).

__strlen   A program sets this pointer to the address of strlen [refer to string(BA_LIB)].

__ulimit   A program sets this pointer to the address of ulimit(BA_OS).

__write   A program sets this pointer to the address of write(BA_OS).

Refer to "System Data Interfaces" later in this chapter for more information.

X-Windows Version 11 Release 4 Library

This section on **libX11** implementation is at Level 2.

THE FACILITIES AND INTERFACES DESCRIBED IN THIS SECTION ARE
OPTIONAL COMPONENTS OF the Intel386 Family Binary Compatibility
Specification.

The X-Windows (X11R4) services library, **libX11**, is optional. If provided, it contains the following routines, along with their assigned virtual addresses. The
libX11 shared library text segments start at address 0xa0800000 and continue
upward within the process virtual address space. The **libX11** shared library
data segments start at address 0xa0c00000 within the process virtual address
space. The **X11R4** document referenced in Chapter 1 gives the interfaces to the
services given below.

Figure 6-4: libX11 Contents

reserved	0xa08008a7
reserved	0xa080086b
reserved	0xa0800889
reserved	0xa0800898
reserved	0xa080085c
reserved	0xa080087a
reserved	0xa08008ac
reserved	0xa0800870
reserved	0xa080088e
reserved	0xa08008b6
reserved	0xa0800a4b
reserved	0xa080025d
reserved	0xa08008a2
reserved	0xa0800866
reserved	0xa0800884
reserved	0xa08008b1
reserved	0xa0800875
reserved	0xa0800893
reserved	0xa080089d

Figure 6-4: libX11 **Contents** (continued)

reserved	0xa0800861
reserved	0xa080087f
XActivateScreenSaver	0xa08005b4
XAddExtension	0xa0800a19
XAddHost	0xa08004c4
XAddHosts	0xa08004ba
XAddPixel	0xa08002b2
XAddToExtensionList	0xa0800a23
XAddToSaveSet	0xa080079e
XAllPlanes	0xa080039d
XAllocClassHint	0xa080099c
XAllocColor	0xa080055a
XAllocColorCells	0xa0800820
XAllocColorPlanes	0xa080080c
XAllocIconSize	0xa08009a1
XAllocNamedColor	0xa080057d
XAllocSizeHints	0xa080098d
XAllocStandardColormap	0xa0800992
XAllocWMHints	0xa0800997
XAllowEvents	0xa0800807
XAutoRepeatOff	0xa08007fd
XAutoRepeatOn	0xa0800802
XBell	0xa08007e9
XBitmapBitOrder	0xa0800348
XBitmapPad	0xa0800343
XBitmapUnit	0xa080034d
XBlackPixel	0xa08003a7
XBlackPixelOfScreen	0xa080031b
XCellsOfScreen	0xa08002e4
XChangeActivePointerGrab	0xa08007cb
XChangeGC	0xa08007c1
XChangeKeyboardControl	0xa08007f8
XChangeKeyboardMapping	0xa08000f5
XChangePointerControl	0xa08007ad
XChangeProperty	0xa08007a8
XChangeSaveSet	0xa08007a3
XChangeWindowAttributes	0xa0800794

Figure 6-4: libX11 **Contents** (continued)

XCheckIfEvent	0xa0800785
XCheckMaskEvent	0xa080077b
XCheckTypedEvent	0xa0800771
XCheckTypedWindowEvent	0xa080076c
XCheckWindowEvent	0xa0800776
XCirculateSubwindows	0xa0800767
XCirculateSubwindowsDown	0xa0800762
XCirculateSubwindowsUp	0xa080075d
XClearArea	0xa080073a
XClearWindow	0xa080073f
XClipBox	0xa08001d1
XCloseDisplay	0xa0800758
XConfigureWindow	0xa08001d6
XConnectionNumber	0xa08003c5
XConvertSelection	0xa080070d
XCopyArea	0xa0800708
XCopyColormapAndFree	0xa0800703
XCopyGC	0xa08006fe
XCopyPlane	0xa08006f9
XCreateBitmapFromData	0xa08006f4
XCreateColormap	0xa08006e0
XCreateFontCursor	0xa08006bd
XCreateGC	0xa08006ea
XCreateGlyphCursor	0xa08006cc
XCreateImage	0xa080051e
XCreatePixmap	0xa08006ef
XCreatePixmapCursor	0xa08006db
XCreatePixmapFromBitmapData	0xa08006c7
XCreateRegion	0xa0800235
XCreateSimpleWindow	0xa08006c2
XCreateWindow	0xa0800032
XDefaultColormap	0xa0800352
XDefaultColormapOfScreen	0xa0800311
XDefaultDepth	0xa0800357
XDefaultDepthOfScreen	0xa080030c
XDefaultGC	0xa08003ac
XDefaultGCOfScreen	0xa0800307

Figure 6-4: libX11 **Contents** (continued)

XDefaultRootWindow	0xa08003b6
XDefaultScreen	0xa08003bb
XDefaultScreenOfDisplay	0xa080032a
XDefaultVisual	0xa08003b1
XDefaultVisualOfScreen	0xa0800302
XDefineCursor	0xa08006ae
XDeleteContext	0xa080084d
XDeleteModifiermapEntry	0xa0800285
XDeleteProperty	0xa08006a9
XDestroyImage	0xa08002c6
XDestroyRegion	0xa08001c2
XDestroySubwindows	0xa08006a4
XDestroyWindow	0xa080069f
XDisableAccessControl	0xa08007da
XDisplayCells	0xa080037a
XDisplayHeight	0xa080038e
XDisplayHeightMM	0xa0800384
XDisplayKeycodes	0xa0800a41
XDisplayMotionBufferSize	0xa0800a3c
XDisplayName	0xa080069a
XDisplayOfScreen	0xa0800325
XDisplayPlanes	0xa080037f
XDisplayString	0xa080035c
XDisplayWidth	0xa0800393
XDisplayWidthMM	0xa0800389
XDoesBackingStore	0xa08002d0
XDoesSaveUnders	0xa08002d5
XDrawArc	0xa0800695
XDrawArcs	0xa0800690
XDrawImageString	0xa0800483
XDrawImageString16	0xa0800479
XDrawLine	0xa080068b
XDrawLines	0xa0800686
XDrawPoint	0xa0800681
XDrawPoints	0xa080067c
XDrawRectangle	0xa0800677
XDrawRectangles	0xa0800672

Figure 6-4: libX11 **Contents** (continued)

XDrawSegments	0xa080066d
XDrawString	0xa080008c
XDrawString16	0xa0800087
XDrawText	0xa0800230
XDrawText16	0xa080022b
XEHeadOfExtensionList	0xa0800a1e
XESetCloseDisplay	0xa080044c
XESetCopyGC	0xa0800465
XESetCreateFont	0xa0800456
XESetCreateGC	0xa080046a
XESetError	0xa080043d
XESetErrorString	0xa0800438
XESetEventToWire	0xa0800442
XESetFlushGC	0xa0800460
XESetFreeFont	0xa0800451
XESetFreeGC	0xa080045b
XESetWireToEvent	0xa0800447
XEmptyRegion	0xa080019a
XEnableAccessControl	0xa08007df
XEqualRegion	0xa0800195
XEventMaskOfScreen	0xa08002cb
XEventsQueued	0xa080024e
XFetchBuffer	0xa08000c8
XFetchBytes	0xa08000c3
XFetchName	0xa0800627
XFillArc	0xa0800618
XFillArcs	0xa0800613
XFillPolygon	0xa080060e
XFillRectangle	0xa0800609
XFillRectangles	0xa0800604
XFindContext	0xa0800852
XFindOnExtensionList	0xa0800a28
XFlush	0xa08005ff
XForceScreenSaver	0xa08005aa
XFree	0xa0800028
XFreeColormap	0xa08005c8
XFreeColors	0xa08005c3

Figure 6-4: `libX11` **Contents** (continued)

XFreeCursor	0xa08005be
XFreeExtensionList	0xa08003d4
XFreeFont	0xa08005f5
XFreeFontInfo	0xa08005cd
XFreeFontNames	0xa08005dc
XFreeFontPath	0xa0800569
XFreeGC	0xa0800753
XFreeModifiermap	0xa08003f7
XFreePixmap	0xa08005b9
XFreeStringList	0xa08009ec
XGContextFromGC	0xa08006d1
XGeometry	0xa080058c
XGetAtomName	0xa0800582
XGetClassHint	0xa0800537
XGetCommand	0xa0800a2d
XGetDefault	0xa0800578
XGetErrorDatabaseText	0xa0800663
XGetErrorText	0xa0800668
XGetFontPath	0xa080056e
XGetFontProperty	0xa0800564
XGetGCValues	0xa080094c
XGetGeometry	0xa080055f
XGetIconName	0xa0800622
XGetIconSizes	0xa0800541
XGetImage	0xa080052d
XGetInputFocus	0xa0800532
XGetKeyboardControl	0xa080050a
XGetKeyboardMapping	0xa08004f6
XGetModifierMapping	0xa08003f2
XGetMotionEvents	0xa0800505
XGetNormalHints	0xa0800546
XGetPixel	0xa08002c1
XGetPointerControl	0xa0800500
XGetPointerMapping	0xa08004fb
XGetRGBColormaps	0xa080095b
XGetScreenSaver	0xa08004ec
XGetSelectionOwner	0xa08004f1

Figure 6-4: libX11 **Contents** (continued)

XGetSizeHints	0xa0800555
XGetStandardColormap	0xa08004e7
XGetSubImage	0xa0800528
XGetTextProperty	0xa0800960
XGetTransientForHint	0xa080053c
XGetVisualInfo	0xa0800046
XGetWMClientMachine	0xa080096f
XGetWMColormapWindows	0xa0800979
XGetWMHints	0xa0800550
XGetWMIconName	0xa080096a
XGetWMName	0xa0800965
XGetWMNormalHints	0xa0800956
XGetWMProtocols	0xa080097e
XGetWMSizeHints	0xa0800951
XGetWindowAttributes	0xa08004e2
XGetWindowProperty	0xa080061d
XGetZoomHints	0xa080054b
XGrabButton	0xa08004dd
XGrabKey	0xa08004d8
XGrabKeyboard	0xa08004d3
XGrabPointer	0xa08004ce
XGrabServer	0xa08004c9
XHeightMMOfScreen	0xa08002ee
XHeightOfScreen	0xa08002f8
XHideStatic	0xa080050f
XHideStatic2	0xa08009ce
XIconifyWindow	0xa0800983
XIfEvent	0xa08004b0
XImageByteOrder	0xa080033e
XInitExtension	0xa080046f
XInsertModifiermapEntry	0xa080028a
XInstallColormap	0xa0800429
XInternAtom	0xa0800424
XIntersectRegion	0xa08001b3
XKeycodeToKeysym	0xa080041f
XKeysymToKeycode	0xa080041a
XKeysymToString	0xa080009b

Figure 6-4: libX11 **Contents** (continued)

XKillClient	0xa08003ed
XLastKnownRequestProcessed	0xa0800334
XListDepths	0xa0800a55
XListExtensions	0xa08003d9
XListFonts	0xa08005e1
XListFontsWithInfo	0xa08005d2
XListHosts	0xa08003e8
XListInstalledColormaps	0xa08003e3
XListPixmapFormats	0xa0800988
XListProperties	0xa08003de
XLoadFont	0xa08006b3
XLoadQueryFont	0xa08005fa
XLookupColor	0xa08003cf
XLookupKeysym	0xa0800415
XLookupString	0xa0800401
XLowerWindow	0xa08003ca
XMapRaised	0xa08002a8
XMapSubwindows	0xa08002a3
XMapWindow	0xa080029e
XMaskEvent	0xa0800299
XMatchVisualInfo	0xa0800041
XMaxCmapsOfScreen	0xa08002da
XMaxRequestSize	0xa0800a32
XMinCmapsOfScreen	0xa08002df
XMoveResizeWindow	0xa0800735
XMoveWindow	0xa0800280
XNewModifiermap	0xa080028f
XNextEvent	0xa080027b
XNextRequest	0xa0800339
XNoOp	0xa08002ad
XOffsetRegion	0xa08001bd
XOpenDisplay	0xa0800276
XParseColor	0xa0800262
XParseGeometry	0xa0800587
XPeekEvent	0xa0800258
XPeekIfEvent	0xa0800253
XPending	0xa0800249

Figure 6-4: libX11 **Contents** (continued)

XPlanesOfScreen	0xa08002e9
XPointInRegion	0xa0800190
XPolygonRegion	0xa080023a
XProtocolRevision	0xa0800366
XProtocolVersion	0xa080036b
XPutBackEvent	0xa0800226
XPutImage	0xa08006e5
XPutPixel	0xa08002bc
XQLength	0xa0800398
XQueryBestCursor	0xa080020d
XQueryBestSize	0xa080021c
XQueryBestStipple	0xa08001fe
XQueryBestTile	0xa08001ef
XQueryColor	0xa0800217
XQueryColors	0xa0800212
XQueryExtension	0xa0800433
XQueryFont	0xa08005eb
XQueryKeymap	0xa0800208
XQueryPointer	0xa0800203
XQueryTextExtents	0xa08001f4
XQueryTextExtents16	0xa08001f9
XQueryTree	0xa08001ea
XRaiseWindow	0xa08001e5
XReadBitmapFile	0xa08001e0
XRebindKeysym	0xa08003fc
XRecolorCursor	0xa08001db
XReconfigureWMWindow	0xa08009a6
XRectInRegion	0xa080018b
XRefreshKeyboardMapping	0xa0800410
XRemoveFromSaveSet	0xa0800799
XRemoveHost	0xa08004bf
XRemoveHosts	0xa08004b5
XReparentWindow	0xa0800181
XResetScreenSaver	0xa08005af
XResizeWindow	0xa080078a
XResourceManagerString	0xa0800a37
XRestackWindows	0xa080017c

Figure 6-4: libX11 **Contents** (continued)

XRootWindow	0xa08003c0
XRootWindowOfScreen	0xa0800320
XRotateBuffers	0xa08000cd
XRotateWindowProperties	0xa0800177
XSaveContext	0xa0800857
XScreenCount	0xa0800375
XScreenNumberOfScreen	0xa0800a14
XScreenOfDisplay	0xa080032f
XSelect	0xa080090b
XSelectInput	0xa0800172
XSendEvent	0xa080016d
XServerVendor	0xa0800370
XSetAccessControl	0xa08007d5
XSetAfterFunction	0xa0800091
XSetArcMode	0xa08005a5
XSetAuthorization	0xa0800a0f
XSetBackground	0xa0800168
XSetClassHint	0xa0800113
XSetClipMask	0xa080015e
XSetClipOrigin	0xa0800159
XSetClipRectangles	0xa0800163
XSetCloseDownMode	0xa08007d0
XSetCommand	0xa0800122
XSetDashes	0xa0800154
XSetErrorHandler	0xa0800645
XSetFillRule	0xa08005a0
XSetFillStyle	0xa080059b
XSetFont	0xa080014a
XSetFontPath	0xa080014f
XSetForeground	0xa0800145
XSetFunction	0xa0800140
XSetGraphicsExposures	0xa0800596
XSetIOErrorHandler	0xa0800640
XSetIconName	0xa08000a5
XSetIconSizes	0xa0800127
XSetInputFocus	0xa0800109
XSetLineAttributes	0xa0800104

Figure 6-4: libX11 **Contents** (continued)

XSetModifierMapping	0xa0800294
XSetNormalHints	0xa080012c
XSetPlaneMask	0xa08000ff
XSetPointerMapping	0xa08000fa
XSetRGBColormaps	0xa08009b5
XSetRegion	0xa08001c7
XSetScreenSaver	0xa08000eb
XSetSelectionOwner	0xa08000f0
XSetSizeHints	0xa080013b
XSetStandardColormap	0xa08000dc
XSetStandardProperties	0xa080011d
XSetState	0xa08000e6
XSetStipple	0xa08000e1
XSetSubwindowMode	0xa0800591
XSetTSOrigin	0xa08000d2
XSetTextProperty	0xa08009bf
XSetTile	0xa08000d7
XSetTransientForHint	0xa0800118
XSetWMClientMachine	0xa08009c9
XSetWMColormapWindows	0xa08009d3
XSetWMHints	0xa0800136
XSetWMIconName	0xa08009c4
XSetWMName	0xa08009ba
XSetWMNormalHints	0xa08009b0
XSetWMProperties	0xa08009d8
XSetWMProtocols	0xa08009dd
XSetWMSizeHints	0xa08009ab
XSetWindowBackground	0xa08007f3
XSetWindowBackgroundPixmap	0xa0800244
XSetWindowBorder	0xa08007e4
XSetWindowBorderPixmap	0xa080023f
XSetWindowBorderWidth	0xa08007ee
XSetWindowColormap	0xa08007c6
XSetZoomHints	0xa0800131
XShrinkRegion	0xa08001b8
XStoreBuffer	0xa08000be
XStoreBytes	0xa08000b9

Figure 6-4: `libX11` **Contents** (continued)

XStoreColor	0xa08000b4
XStoreColors	0xa08000af
XStoreName	0xa080010e
XStoreNamedColor	0xa08000aa
XStringListToTextProperty	0xa08009e2
XStringToKeysym	0xa08000a0
XSubImage	0xa08002b7
XSubtractRegion	0xa08001a4
XSync	0xa080074e
XSynchronize	0xa0800267
XTestFakeInput	0xa0800938
XTestFlush	0xa0800924
XTestGetInput	0xa0800929
XTestMovePointer	0xa0800915
XTestPressButton	0xa080091a
XTestPressKey	0xa080091f
XTestQueryInputSize	0xa0800933
XTestReset	0xa080093d
XTestStartSimulation	0xa0800942
XTestStopInput	0xa080092e
XTestStopSimulation	0xa0800947
XTextExtents	0xa080047e
XTextExtents16	0xa0800474
XTextPropertyToStringList	0xa08009e7
XTextWidth	0xa0800082
XTextWidth16	0xa080007d
XTranslateCoordinates	0xa0800078
XUndefineCursor	0xa0800073
XUngrabButton	0xa080006e
XUngrabKey	0xa0800064
XUngrabKeyboard	0xa0800069
XUngrabPointer	0xa080005f
XUngrabServer	0xa080005a
XUninstallColormap	0xa0800055
XUnionRectWithRegion	0xa08001cc
XUnionRegion	0xa08001a9
XUnloadFont	0xa08006b8

Figure 6-4: libX11 **Contents** (continued)

XUnmapSubwindows	0xa0800050
XUnmapWindow	0xa080004b
XVendorRelease	0xa0800361
XVisualIDFromVisual	0xa0800a46
XWMGeometry	0xa08009f1
XWarpPointer	0xa080003c
XWhitePixel	0xa08003a2
XWhitePixelOfScreen	0xa0800316
XWidthMMOfScreen	0xa08002f3
XWidthOfScreen	0xa08002fd
XWindowEvent	0xa0800037
XWithdrawWindow	0xa08009f6
XWriteBitmapFile	0xa080002d
XXorRegion	0xa080019f
XauDisposeAuth	0xa08009fb
XauFileName	0xa0800a00
XauGetAuthByAddr	0xa0800a05
XauReadAuth	0xa0800a0a
Xpermalloc	0xa0800834
XrmDestroyDatabase	0xa0800a5a
XrmGetFileDatabase	0xa080064f
XrmGetResource	0xa0800659
XrmGetStringDatabase	0xa0800573
XrmInitialize	0xa0800654
XrmMergeDatabases	0xa080064a
XrmParseCommand	0xa0800848
XrmPutFileDatabase	0xa0800005
XrmPutLineResource	0xa0800839
XrmPutResource	0xa080000f
XrmPutStringResource	0xa080000a
XrmQGetResource	0xa0800000
XrmQGetSearchList	0xa080001e
XrmQGetSearchResource	0xa0800019
XrmQPutResource	0xa0800014
XrmQPutStringResource	0xa080083e
XrmQuarkToString	0xa0800825
XrmStringToBindingQuarkList	0xa0800843

Figure 6-4: libX11 **Contents** (continued)

XrmStringToQuark	0xa080082f
XrmStringToQuarkList	0xa0800023
XrmUniqueQuark	0xa080082a
_Reverse_Bytes	0xa0800a8c
_XAllocID	0xa080026c
_XAllocScratch	0xa0800221
_XBytesReadable	0xa080071c
_XConnectDisplay	0xa0800730
_XDefaultError	0xa080063b
_XDefaultIOError	0xa0800a5f
_XDisconnectDisplay	0xa0800749
_XEatData	0xa0800a64
_XEnq	0xa0800712
_XError	0xa0800717
_XEventToWire	0xa0800631
_XEventsQueued	0xa0800780
_XFlush	0xa080081b
_XFlushGCCache	0xa08007b7
_XFreeDisplayStructure	0xa0800744
_XFreeExtData	0xa08005e6
_XFreeKeyBindings	0xa0800a69
_XFreeQ	0xa0800a6e
_XGenerateGCList	0xa08006d6
_XGetBitsPerPixel	0xa08004a6
_XGetHostname	0xa08008f2
_XGetScanlinePad	0xa0800519
_XIOError	0xa0800636
_XInitImageFuncPtrs	0xa080048d
_XMakeStreamsConnection	0xa0800a73
_XProcessWindowAttributes	0xa080078f
_XRead	0xa0800811
_XReadEvents	0xa08004ab
_XReadPad	0xa08005d7
_XReply	0xa0800816
_XScreenOfWindow	0xa0800a78
_XSend	0xa08007b2
_XSendClientPrefix	0xa0800721

Figure 6-4: libX11 **Contents** (continued)

_XSetClipRectangles	0xa0800186
_XSetImage	0xa0800514
_XSetLastRequestRead	0xa0800a91
_XSyncFunction	0xa0800096
_XUnknownNativeEvent	0xa080062c
_XUnknownWireEvent	0xa080042e
_XUpdateGCCache	0xa08007bc
_XVIDtoVisual	0xa0800523
_XWaitForReadable	0xa0800726
_XWaitForWritable	0xa080072b
_XWireToEvent	0xa0800271
_XrmGetResourceName	0xa0800a7d
reserved	0xa08008d4
reserved	0xa08008cf
reserved	0xa0800a82
bcmp	0xa0800901
bcopy	0xa0800906
bzero	0xa08008fc
reserved	0xa08001ae
ffs	0xa08008f7
gettimeofday	0xa08008ed
index	0xa08008e8
insque	0xa08008de
nameserver	0xa0800a87
pollselect	0xa0800a50
random	0xa08008ca
remque	0xa08008d9
rindex	0xa08008e3
srandom	0xa08008c5
usleep	0xa08008bb
reserved	0xa0c00378
XErrorList	0xa0c00298
XErrorListSize	0xa0c00374
XTestFakeAckType	0xa0c004dc
XTestInputActionType	0xa0c004d8
XrmQString	0xa0c00238
_XErrorFunction	0xa0c00180

Figure 6-4: libX11 **Contents** (continued)

_XHeadOfDisplayList	0xa0c00190
_XIOErrorFunction	0xa0c0017c
_Xdebug	0xa0c00184
_libX__ctype	0xa0c00040
_libX__iob	0xa0c000e0
_libX_abs	0xa0c00018
_libX_alarm	0xa0c00098
_libX_atoi	0xa0c000c8
_libX_calloc	0xa0c00058
_libX_chmod	0xa0c000b4
_libX_close	0xa0c000b0
_libX_daylight	0xa0c00104
_libX_errno	0xa0c00118
_libX_exit	0xa0c00050
_libX_fclose	0xa0c00014
_libX_fcntl	0xa0c0003c
_libX_fgets	0xa0c0000c
_libX_fopen	0xa0c00010
_libX_fprintf	0xa0c000dc
_libX_fputs	0xa0c00020
_libX_free	0xa0c000f4
_libX_fscanf	0xa0c00004
_libX_fwrite	0xa0c0001c
_libX_getenv	0xa0c00030
_libX_getpwnam	0xa0c0002c
_libX_getpwuid	0xa0c00024
_libX_getuid	0xa0c00028
_libX_grantpt	0xa0c000d0
_libX_ioctl	0xa0c00034
_libX_link	0xa0c000b8
_libX_malloc	0xa0c000f8
_libX_memccpy	0xa0c00048
_libX_memchr	0xa0c00044
_libX_memcmp	0xa0c00120
_libX_memcpy	0xa0c00124
_libX_memset	0xa0c0011c
_libX_open	0xa0c000d8

Figure 6-4: libX11 **Contents** (continued)

_libX_perror	0xa0c000d4
_libX_poll	0xa0c000e4
_libX_ptsname	0xa0c000bc
_libX_rand	0xa0c000f0
_libX_read	0xa0c000ac
_libX_realloc	0xa0c00054
_libX_signal	0xa0c0009c
_libX_sprintf	0xa0c000c4
_libX_srand	0xa0c000ec
_libX_sscanf	0xa0c00008
_libX_strcat	0xa0c000a8
_libX_strchr	0xa0c00100
_libX_strcmp	0xa0c0004c
_libX_strcpy	0xa0c00038
_libX_strlen	0xa0c000a0
_libX_strncpy	0xa0c00110
_libX_strrchr	0xa0c000fc
_libX_t_accept	0xa0c00074
_libX_t_alloc	0xa0c0008c
_libX_t_bind	0xa0c00088
_libX_t_close	0xa0c00078
_libX_t_connect	0xa0c0006c
_libX_t_errno	0xa0c0007c
_libX_t_error	0xa0c00090
_libX_t_free	0xa0c00070
_libX_t_listen	0xa0c00080
_libX_t_look	0xa0c00084
_libX_t_open	0xa0c00094
_libX_t_rcv	0xa0c00068
_libX_t_snd	0xa0c00064
_libX_t_snddis	0xa0c00060
_libX_t_unbind	0xa0c0005c
_libX_time	0xa0c0010c
_libX_times	0xa0c00128
_libX_timezone	0xa0c00108
_libX_ulimit	0xa0c000e8
_libX_uname	0xa0c00114

Figure 6-4: libX11 **Contents** (continued)

```
        _libX_unlink              0xa0c000c0
        _libX_unlockpt            0xa0c000cc
        _libX_write               0xa0c000a4
        reserved                  0xa0c004ec
        reserved                  0xa0c003dc
```

System Data Interfaces

Standard header files that describe system data are available for C application developers to use. These files are referred to by their name in angle brackets: <name.h> and <sys/name.h>. Included in these headers are macro definitions, data definitions, and function declarations. The parts of the header files specified in the ANSI C standard are the only parts available to strictly-conforming ANSI C applications.

Some of the header files in the following section define interfaces directly available to applications, and those interfaces will be common to systems on all processors. Other header files show specific implementations of standard interfaces on the Intel386 architecture. The iBCS does not distinguish between these files. It gives data definitions to promote binary application portability, not to repeat source interface definitions available elsewhere. System providers and application developers should use the iBCS to supplement — not to replace — source interface definition documents.

Some type and data definitions appear in multiple headers. Special definitions are included in the headers to avoid conflicts.

The application execution environment presents the interfaces described below, but the iBCS does not require the presence of the header files themselves. In other words, a iBCS-conforming system is not required to provide an application development environment. The specific definitions are not guaranteed to exist in a particular file or in any particular order. The size (and type) of individual data elements and ordering and size (and type) of individual elements within structures must be as specified in the following sections for any iBCS-conforming system.

Data Definitions

This section contains standard header files that describe system data. These files are referred to by their names in angle brackets: <name.h> and <sys/name.h>. Included in these headers are macro definitions and data definitions.

The data objects described in this section are part of the interface between an iBCS-conforming application and the underlying iBCS-conforming system where it will run. While an iBCS-conforming system must provide these interfaces, it is not required to contain the actual header files referenced here. Programmers should observe that the sources of the structures defined in these headers are defined in the **SVID**.

ANSI C serves as the iBCS reference programming language, and data definitions are specified in ANSI C format. The C language is used here as a convenient notation. Using a C language description of these data objects does *not* preclude their use by other programming languages.

NOTE Although the ANSI C language is used as the reference programming language, it may not be possible to produce strictly ANSI C conforming application programs using these header files.

Figure 6-5: <ctype.h>

```
#define _U    01
#define _L    02
#define _N    04
#define _S    010
#define _P    020
#define _C    040
#define _B    0100
#define _X    0200

extern unsigned char    _ctype[];

#define isalpha(c)  ((_ctype+1)[c]&(_U|_L))
#define isupper(c)  ((_ctype+1)[c]&_U)
#define islower(c)  ((_ctype+1)[c]&_L)
#define isdigit(c)  ((_ctype+1)[c]&_N)
#define isxdigit(c) ((_ctype+1)[c]&_X)
#define isalnum(c)  ((_ctype+1)[c]&(_U|_L|_N))
#define isspace(c)  ((_ctype+1)[c]&_S)
#define ispunct(c)  ((_ctype+1)[c]&_P)
#define isprint(c)  ((_ctype+1)[c]&(_P|_U|_L|_N|_B))
#define isgraph(c)  ((_ctype+1)[c]&(_P|_U|_L|_N))
#define iscntrl(c)  ((_ctype+1)[c]&_C)
#define isascii(c)  (!((c)&~0177))
#define _toupper(c) ((_ctype+258)[c])
#define _tolower(c) ((_ctype+258)[c])
#define toascii(c)  ((c)&0177)
```

Figure 6-6: <dirent.h>

```
#define MAXNAMLEN          512
#define DIRBUF             1048

typedef struct {
        int          dd_fd;
        int          dd_loc;
        int          dd_size;
        char         *dd_buf;
} DIR;

struct dirent {
        long                 d_ino;
        off_t                d_off;
        unsigned short       d_reclen;
        char                 d_name[1];
};
```

Figure 6-7: `<errno.h>`, Part 1 of 3

```
#define EPERM          1
#define ENOENT         2
#define ESRCH          3
#define EINTR          4
#define EIO            5
#define ENXIO          6
#define E2BIG          7
#define ENOEXEC        8
#define EBADF          9
#define ECHILD         10
#define EAGAIN         11
#define ENOMEM         12
#define EACCES         13
#define EFAULT         14
#define ENOTBLK        15
#define EBUSY          16
#define EEXIST         17
#define EXDEV          18
#define ENODEV         19
#define ENOTDIR        20
#define EISDIR         21
#define EINVAL         22
#define ENFILE         23
#define EMFILE         24
#define ENOTTY         25
#define ETXTBSY        26
#define EFBIG          27
#define ENOSPC         28
#define ESPIPE         29
#define EROFS          30
#define EMLINK         31
#define EPIPE          32
```

Figure 6-8: `<errno.h>`, Part 2 of 3

```
#define EDOM            33
#define ERANGE          34
#define ENOMSG          35
#define EIDRM           36
#define ECHRNG          37
#define EL2NSYNC        38
#define EL3HLT          39
#define EL3RST          40
#define ELNRNG          41
#define EUNATCH         42
#define ENOCSI          43
#define EL2HLT          44
#define EDEADLK         45
#define ENOLCK          46
#define ENOSTR          60
#define ENODATA         61
#define ETIME           62
#define ENOSR           63
#define ENONET          64
#define ENOPKG          65
#define EREMOTE         66
#define ENOLINK         67
#define EADV            68
#define ESRMNT          69
#define ECOMM           70
#define EPROTO          71
#define EMULTIHOP       74
#define ELBIN           75
#define EDOTDOT         76
#define EBADMSG         77
#define ENAMETOOLONG    78
#define EOVERFLOW       79      /* RESERVED */
```

Figure 6-9: <errno.h>, **Part 3 of 3**

```
#define ENOTUNIQ        80
#define EBADFD          81
#define EREMCHG         82
#define EEILSEQ         88        /* RESERVED */
#define ENOSYS          89
#define ELOOP           90
#define EWOULDBLOCK     90        /* Level 2 */
#define ERESTART        91
#define ESTRPIPE        92
#define ENOTEMPTY       93
#define EUSERS          94
#define ESTALE          151       /* RESERVED */
#define EIORESID        500       /* RESERVED */

extern int errno;
```

Figure 6-10: `<fcntl.h>`, Part 1 of 2

```
#define O_RDONLY        0
#define O_WRONLY        1
#define O_RDWR          2
#define O_NDELAY        0x04
#define O_APPEND        0x08
#define O_SYNC          0x10
#define O_NONBLOCK      0x80
#define O_CREAT         0x100
#define O_TRUNC         0x200
#define O_EXCL          0x400
#define O_NOCTTY        0x800

#define F_DUPFD         0
#define F_GETFD         1
#define F_SETFD         2
#define F_GETFL         3
#define F_SETFL         4
#define F_GETLK         5
#define F_SETLK         6
#define F_SETLKW        7
```

Figure 6-11: <fcntl.h>, **Part 2 of 2**

```
typedef struct flock {
        short           l_type;
        short           l_whence;
        long            l_start;
        long            l_len;
        short           l_sysid;
        short           l_pid;
} flock_t;

#define F_RDLCK         01
#define F_WRLCK         02
#define F_UNLCK         03


#define O_ACCMODE       3
#define FD_CLOEXEC      1
```

Figure 6-12: <sys/fp.h>

```
#define FP_NO           0
#define FP_SW           1
#define FP_HW           2
#define FP_287          2
#define FP_387          3
```

Figure 6-13: `<ftw.h>`

```
#define FTW_F        0
#define FTW_D        1
#define FTW_DNR      2
#define FTW_NS       3
```

Figure 6-14: `<grp.h>`

```
struct group {
        char    *gr_name;
        char    *gr_passwd;
        int     gr_gid;
        char    **gr_mem;
};
```

Figure 6-15: <ieeefp.h>

```
struct _fpstackframe {
        long                    signo;
        long                    regs[SS+1];
        struct _fpstate         *fpsp;
        char                    *wsp;
};

struct _fpreg {
        unsigned short          significand[4];
        unsigned short          exponent;
};

struct _fpstate {
        unsigned long           cw,
                                sw,
                                tag,
                                ipoff,
                                cssel,
                                dataoff,
                                datasel;
        struct _fpreg           _st[8];
        unsigned long           status;
};
```

Figure 6-16: <sys/ipc.h>

```
struct ipc_perm {
        ushort          uid;
        ushort          gid;
        ushort          cuid;
        ushort          cgid;
        ushort          mode;
        ushort          seq;
        key_t           key;
};

#define IPC_CREAT    0001000
#define IPC_EXCL     0002000
#define IPC_NOWAIT   0004000

#define IPC_PRIVATE  (key_t)0

#define IPC_RMID            0
#define IPC_SET             1
#define IPC_STAT            2
```

Figure 6-17: `<limits.h>`, **Part 1 of 2**

```
#define CHAR_BIT         8
#define SCHAR_MIN        (-128)
#define SCHAR_MAX        127
#define UCHAR_MAX        255
#define CHAR_MIN         0
#define CHAR_MAX         255
#define SHRT_MIN         (-32768)
#define SHRT_MAX         32767
#define USHRT_MAX        65535
#define INT_MIN          (-2147483647-1)
#define INT_MAX          2147483647
#define UINT_MAX         4294967295
#define LONG_MIN         (-2147483647-1)
#define LONG_MAX         2147483647
#define ULONG_MAX        4294967295
#define WORD_BIT         32
#define LONG_BIT         32

#define DBL_DIG          15
#define DBL_MAX          1.7976931348623157e+308
#define DBL_MIN          2.2250738585072014e-308
#define FLT_DIG          6
#define FLT_MAX          3.4028234663852886e+38
#define FLT_MIN          1.17549435082228755e-38
```

Figure 6-18: `<limits.h>`, **Part 2 of 2**

```
#define CLK_TCK          100
#define ARG_MAX          5120
#define LINK_MAX         1000
#define PATH_MAX         256
#define PIPE_BUF         5120
#define PIPE_MAX         5120
#define PASS_MAX         8
#define CHILD_MAX        25
#define SYS_NMLN         9
#define UID_MAX          60000

#define FCHR_MAX         1048576
```

Figure 6-19: `<sys/lock.h>`

```
#define UNLOCK           0
#define PROCLOCK         1
#define TXTLOCK          2
#define DATLOCK          4
```

Figure 6-20: `<math.h>`

```
typedef union _h_val {
        unsigned long        i[2];
        double               d;
} _h_val;

extern const _h_val __huge_val;
#define HUGE_VAL     __huge_val.d
```

Figure 6-21: `<sys/mount.h>`

```
#define MS_RDONLY        0x01
#define MS_FSS           0x02
#define MS_DATA          0x04
#define MS_CACHE         0x08
```

Figure 6-22: `<sys/msg.h>`

```
#define MSG_NOERROR           010000

struct msqid_ds {
        struct ipc_perm      msg_perm;
        struct msg      *msg_first;
        struct msg      *msg_last;
        ushort          msg_cbytes;
        ushort          msg_qnum;
        ushort          msg_qbytes;
        ushort          msg_lspid;
        ushort          msg_lrpid;
        time_t          msg_stime;
        time_t          msg_rtime;
        time_t          msg_ctime;
};

struct msg {
        struct msg      *msg_next;
        long            msg_type;
        short           msg_ts;
        short           msg_spot;
};
```

Figure 6-23: <sys/param.h>

```
#define MAXPID          30000
#define MAXUID          60000
#define MAXLINK         1000

#define CANBSIZ         256
#define HZ              100
#define TICK            10000000

#define NCARGS          5120
#define NOFILES_MIN     20
#define NOFILES_MAX     100

#define NBPSCTR         512

#define MAXPATHLEN      1024
#define MAXSYMLINKS     20
#define MAXNAMELEN      256

#define NADDR           13

#define PIPE_MAX        5120

#define NBBY            8

#define DEV_BSIZE       512
#define MAXFRAG         8
```

Figure 6-24: `<poll.h>`

```
struct pollfd {
        int     fd;
        short  events;
        short  revents;
};

#define POLLIN          0x0001
#define POLLPRI         0x0002
#define POLLOUT         0x0004
#define POLLERR         0x0008
#define POLLHUP         0x0010
#define POLLNVAL        0x0020
```

Figure 6-25: `<pwd.h>`

```
struct passwd {
        char            *pw_name;
        char            *pw_passwd;
        int             pw_uid;
        int             pw_gid;
        char            *pw_age;
        char            *pw_comment;
        char            *pw_gecos;
        char            *pw_dir;
        char            *pw_shell;
};
```

Figure 6-26: `<sys/reg.h>`

```
#define SS          18
#define UESP        17
#define EFL         16
#define CS          15
#define EIP         14
#define ERR         13
#define TRAPNO      12
#define EAX         11
#define ECX         10
#define EDX          9
#define EBX          8
#define ESP          7
#define EBP          6
#define ESI          5
#define EDI          4
#define DS           3
#define ES           2
#define FS           1
#define GS           0
```

Figure 6-27: `<search.h>`

```
typedef enum { FIND, ENTER } ACTION;
typedef struct entry { char *key; void *data; } ENTRY;
typedef enum { preorder, postorder, endorder, leaf } VISIT;
```

Figure 6-28: `<sys/sem.h>`

```
#define SEM_UNDO    010000
#define GETNCNT     3
#define GETPID      4
#define GETVAL      5
#define GETALL      6
#define GETZCNT     7
#define SETVAL      8
#define SETALL      9

struct semid_ds {
        struct ipc_perm     sem_perm;
        struct sem          *sem_base;
        ushort              sem_nsems;
        time_t              sem_otime;
        time_t              sem_ctime;
};

struct sem {
        ushort      semval;
        short       sempid;
        ushort      semncnt;
        ushort      semzcnt;
};

struct sembuf {
        ushort      sem_num;
        short       sem_op;
        short       sem_flg;
};
```

Figure 6-29: `<setjmp.h>`

```
#define _SIGJBLEN          8
#define _JBLEN             6

typedef int   jmp_buf[_JBLEN];
typedef int   sigjmp_buf[_SIGJBLEN];
```

Figure 6-30: `<sys/shm.h>`

```
#define SHMLBA            (((1)*1024)<<12)

#define SHM_RDONLY        010000
#define SHM_RND           020000

struct shmid_ds {
        struct ipc_perm        shm_perm;
        int                    shm_segsz;
        struct region          *shm_reg;
        char                   pad[4];
        ushort                 shm_lpid;
        ushort                 shm_cpid;
        ushort                 shm_nattch;
        ushort                 shm_cnattch;
        time_t                 shm_atime;
        time_t                 shm_dtime;
        time_t                 shm_ctime;
};
```

Figure 6-31: `<signal.h>`, **Part 1 of 2**

```
#define SIGHUP        1
#define SIGINT        2
#define SIGQUIT       3
#define SIGILL        4
#define SIGTRAP       5
#define SIGIOT        6
#define SIGABRT       6
#define SIGEMT        7
#define SIGFPE        8
#define SIGKILL       9
#define SIGBUS        10
#define SIGSEGV       11
#define SIGSYS        12
#define SIGPIPE       13
#define SIGALRM       14
#define SIGTERM       15
#define SIGUSR1       16
#define SIGUSR2       17
#define SIGCLD        18
#define SIGCHLD       18
#define SIGPWR        19
#define SIGWINCH      20
#define SIGPOLL       22
```

Figure 6-32: `<signal.h>`, **Part 2 of 2**

```
#define SIG_DFL            (void(*)())0
#define SIG_ERR            (void(*)())-1
#define SIG_IGN            (void(*)())1
#define SIG_HOLD           (void(*)())2

#define SIG_SETMASK        0
#define SIG_BLOCK          1
#define SIG_UNBLOCK        2

typedef long       sigset_t;

struct sigaction {
       void        (*sa_handler)();
       sigset_t    sa_mask;
       int         sa_flags;
};

#define SA_NOCLDSTOP       1
```

Figure 6-33: <sys/stat.h>, **Part 1 of 2**

```
struct stat {
        dev_t           st_dev;
        ushort          st_ino;
        ushort          st_mode;
        short           st_nlink;
        ushort          st_uid;
        ushort          st_gid;
        dev_t           st_rdev;
        off_t           st_size;
        time_t          st_atime;
        time_t          st_mtime;
        time_t          st_ctime;
};
```

Figure 6-34: `<sys/stat.h>`, **Part 2 of 2**

```
#define S_IFMT              0xF000
#define S_IFIFO             0x1000
#define S_IFCHR             0x2000
#define S_IFDIR             0x4000
#define S_IFBLK             0x6000
#define S_IFREG             0x8000
#define S_IFSOCK            0xC000

#define S_ISUID             0x800
#define S_ISGID             0x400
#define S_ISVTX             0x200

#define S_IRWXU             00700
#define S_IRUSR             00400
#define S_IWUSR             00200
#define S_IXUSR             00100
#define S_IRWXG             00070
#define S_IRGRP             00040
#define S_IWGRP             00020
#define S_IXGRP             00010
#define S_IRWXO             00007
#define S_IROTH             00004
#define S_IWOTH             00002
#define S_IXOTH             00001

#define S_ISFIFO(mode)      ((mode&S_IFMT) == S_IFIFO)
#define S_ISCHR(mode)       ((mode&S_IFMT) == S_IFCHR)
#define S_ISDIR(mode)       ((mode&S_IFMT) == S_IFDIR)
#define S_ISBLK(mode)       ((mode&S_IFMT) == S_IFBLK)
#define S_ISREG(mode)       ((mode&S_IFMT) == S_IFREG)
#define S_ISSOCK(mode)      ((mode&S_IFMT) == S_IFSOCK)
```

Figure 6-35: `<sys/statfs.h>`

```
typedef struct statfs {
        short           f_fstyp;
        long            f_bsize;
        long            f_frsize;
        long            f_blocks;
        long            f_bfree;
        long            f_files;
        long            f_ffree;
        char            f_fname[6];
        char            f_fpack[6];
};
```

Figure 6-36: `<stddef.h>`

```
#define NULL            0

#define offsetof(s, m)  (size_t)(&(((s *)0)->m))
```

Figure 6-37: <stdio.h>, **Part 1 of 2**

```
typedef long              fpos_t;

#define NULL              0

#define BUFSIZ            1024

#define _NFILE           60

#define _IOFBF           0000
#define _IOLBF           0100
#define _IONBF           0004
#define _IOEOF           0020
#define _IOERR           0040

#define EOF              (-1)

#define FOPEN_MAX        _NFILE

#define L_ctermid        9
#define L_cuserid        9
#define P_tmpdir         "/usr/tmp/"
#define L_tmpnam         (sizeof(P_tmpdir) + 15)

#define stdin            (&_iob[0])
#define stdout           (&_iob[1])
#define stderr           (&_iob[2])
```

Figure 6-38: <stdio.h>**, Part 2 of 2**

```
typedef struct {
        int             _cnt;
        unsigned char   *_ptr;
        unsigned char   *_base;
        char            _flag;
        char            _file;
} FILE;

extern FILE             _iob[_NFILE];

#define clearerr(p) ((void)((p)->_flag &= ~(_IOERR | _IOEOF)))
#define feof(p)     ((p)->_flag & _IOEOF)
#define ferror(p)   ((p)->_flag & _IOERR)
#define fileno(p)   (p)->_file
```

Figure 6-39: `<stropts.h>`, **Part 1 of 3**

```
#define RNORM          0x000
#define RMSGD          0x001
#define RMSGN          0x002

#define FLUSHR         0x01
#define FLUSHW         0x02
#define FLUSHRW        0x03

#define S_INPUT        0x0001
#define S_HIPRI        0x0002
#define S_OUTPUT       0x0004
#define S_MSG          0x0008

#define RS_HIPRI       0x01

#define MORECTL        1
#define MOREDATA       2
```

Figure 6-40: `<stropts.h>`, Part 2 of 3

```
#define STR                    ('S'<<8)
#define I_NREAD                (STR|01)
#define I_PUSH                 (STR|02)
#define I_POP                  (STR|03)
#define I_LOOK                 (STR|04)
#define I_FLUSH                (STR|05)
#define I_SRDOPT               (STR|06)
#define I_GRDOPT               (STR|07)
#define I_STR                  (STR|010)
#define I_SETSIG               (STR|011)
#define I_GETSIG               (STR|012)
#define I_FIND                 (STR|013)
#define I_LINK                 (STR|014)
#define I_UNLINK               (STR|015)
#define I_PEEK                 (STR|017)
#define I_FDINSERT             (STR|020)
#define I_SENDFD               (STR|021)
#define I_RECVFD               (STR|016)

struct strioctl {
        int     ic_cmd;
        int     ic_timout;
        int     ic_len;
        char    *ic_dp;
};
```

Figure 6-41: `<stropts.h>`, **Part 3 of 3**

```
struct strbuf {
        int     maxlen;
        int     len;
        char    *buf;
};

struct strpeek {
        struct strbuf           ctlbuf;
        struct strbuf           databuf;
        long                    flags;
};

struct strfdinsert {
        struct strbuf           ctlbuf;
        struct strbuf           databuf;
        long                    flags;
        int                     fildes;
        int                     offset;
};

struct strrecvfd {
        int                     fd;
        unsigned short          uid;
        unsigned short          gid;
        char                    fill[8];
};
```

Figure 6-42: `<sys/sysi86.h>`

```
#define SI86FPHW          40
```

Figure 6-43: `<termios.h>`, **Part 1 of 11**

```
#define NCC                    8
#define NCCS                  13


typedef unsigned short       tcflag_t;
typedef unsigned char        cc_t;
typedef unsigned long        speed_t;


struct termio {
        unsigned short       c_iflag;
        unsigned short       c_oflag;
        unsigned short       c_cflag;
        unsigned short       c_lflag;
        char          c_line;
        unsigned charc_cc[NCC];
};


struct termios {
        tcflag_t      c_iflag;
        tcflag_t      c_oflag;
        tcflag_t      c_cflag;
        tcflag_t      c_lflag;
        char          c_line;
        cc_t          c_cc[NCCS];
        char          c_ispeed;
        char          c_ospeed;
};
```

Figure 6-44: `<termios.h>`, Part 2 of 11

```
#define VINTR       0
#define VQUIT       1
#define VERASE      2
#define VKILL       3
#define VEOF        4
#define VEOL        5
#define VEOL2       6
#define VMIN        4
#define VTIME       5
#define VSWTCH      7
#define VSUSP      10
#define VSTART     11
#define VSTOP      12
```

Figure 6-45: <termios.h>, **Part 3 of 11**

```
#define CNUL       0
#define CDEL       0377
#define CESC       '\\'
#define CINTR      0177
#define CQUIT      034
#define CERASE     '#'
#define CKILL      '@'
#define CSTART     021
#define CSTOP      023
#define CSWTCH     032
#define CNSWTCH    0
#define CSUSP      032
```

Figure 6-46: `<termios.h>`, **Part 4 of 11**

```
#define IGNBRK          0000001
#define BRKINT          0000002
#define IGNPAR          0000004
#define PARMRK          0000010
#define INPCK           0000020
#define ISTRIP          0000040
#define INLCR           0000100
#define IGNCR           0000200
#define ICRNL           0000400
#define IUCLC           0001000
#define IXON            0002000
#define IXANY           0004000
#define IXOFF           0010000
#define IMAXBEL         0020000      /* RESERVED */
#define DOSMODE         0100000
```

Figure 6-47: `<termios.h>`, **Part 5 of 11**

```
#define OPOST              0000001
#define OLCUC              0000002
#define ONLCR              0000004
#define OCRNL              0000010
#define ONOCR              0000020
#define ONLRET             0000040
#define OFILL              0000100
#define OFDEL              0000200
#define NLDLY              0000400
#define NL0                0
#define NL1                0000400
#define CRDLY              0003000
#define CR0                0
#define CR1                0001000
#define CR2                0002000
#define CR3                0003000
#define TABDLY             0014000
```

Figure 6-48: `<termios.h>`, Part 6 of 11

```
#define TAB0              0
#define TAB1              0004000
#define TAB2              0010000
#define TAB3              0014000
#define BSDLY             0020000
#define BS0               0
#define BS1               0020000
#define VTDLY             0040000
#define VT0               0
#define VT1               0040000
#define FFDLY             0100000
#define FF0               0
#define FF1               0100000
```

Figure 6-49: `<termios.h>`, **Part 7 of 11**

```
#define CBAUD       0000017
#define CSIZE       0000060
#define CS5         0
#define CS6         0000020
#define CS7         0000040
#define CS8         0000060
#define CSTOPB      0000100
#define CREAD       0000200
#define PARENB      0000400
#define PARODD      0001000
#define HUPCL       0002000
#define CLOCAL      0004000
#define RCV1EN      0010000
#define XMT1EN      0020000
#define LOBLK       0040000
#define XCLUDE      0100000
```

Figure 6-50: `<termios.h>`, Part 8 of 11

```
#define ISIG            0000001
#define ICANON          0000002
#define XCASE           0000004
#define ECHO            0000010
#define ECHOE           0000020
#define ECHOK           0000040
#define ECHONL          0000100
#define NOFLSH          0000200
#define IEXTEN          0000400
#define TOSTOP          0001000

/* Bits 10-15 (0176000) in the c_lflag field are RESERVED */
```

Figure 6-51: `<termios.h>`, **Part 9 of 11**

```
/*
#define XIOC              ('x'<<8) Level 2
*/
#define XIOC              (('i'<<8)|('X'<<16))
#define XCGETA            (XIOC|1)
#define XCSETA            (XIOC|2)
#define XCSETAW           (XIOC|3)
#define XCSETAF           (XIOC|4)

#define TIOC              ('T'<<8)

#define TCGETA            (TIOC|1)
#define TCSETA            (TIOC|2)
#define TCSETAW           (TIOC|3)
#define TCSETAF           (TIOC|4)
#define TCSBRK            (TIOC|5)
#define TCXONC            (TIOC|6)
#define TCFLSH            (TIOC|7)

#define TIOCGWINSZ        (TIOC|104)
#define TIOCSWINSZ        (TIOC|103)
```

Figure 6-52: `<termios.h>`, Part 10 of 11

```
#define TCSANOW            XCSETA
#define TCSADRAIN          XCSETAW
#define TCSAFLUSH          XCSETAF
#define TCSADFLUSH         XCSETAF

#define TCIFLUSH           0
#define TCOFLUSH           1
#define TCIOFLUSH          2

#define TCOOFF             0
#define TCOON              1
#define TCIOFF             2
#define TCION              3
```

Figure 6-53: `<termios.h>`, Part 11 of 11

```
#define B0                              0
#define B50                             1
#define B75                             2
#define B110                            3
#define B134                            4
#define B150                            5
#define B200                            6
#define B300                            7
#define B600                            8
#define B1200                           9
#define B1800                           10
#define B2400                           11
#define B4800                           12
#define B9600                           13
#define B19200                          14
#define B38400                          15

struct winsize {
        unsigned short          ws_row;
        unsigned short          ws_col;
        unsigned short          ws_xpixel;
        unsigned short          ws_ypixel;
};
```

Figure 6-54: <sys/time.h>

```
typedef long clock_t;
typedef long time_t;

struct tm {
        int     tm_sec;
        int     tm_min;
        int     tm_hour;
        int     tm_mday;
        int     tm_mon;
        int     tm_year;
        int     tm_wday;
        int     tm_yday;
        int     tm_isdst;
};

extern char *tzname[2];

#define CLK_TCK             100

extern long timezone;
extern int daylight;
```

Figure 6-55: <sys/times.h>

```
struct tms {
        time_t          tms_utime;
        time_t          tms_stime;
        time_t          tms_cutime;
        time_t          tms_cstime;
};
```

Figure 6-56: `<sys/tiuser.h>`, **Error Return Values**

```
#define TBADADDR        1
#define TBADOPT         2
#define TACCES          3
#define TBADF           4
#define TNOADDR         5
#define TOUTSTATE       6
#define TBADSEQ         7
#define TSYSERR         8
#define TLOOK           9
#define TBADDATA        10
#define TBUFOVFLW       11
#define TFLOW           12
#define TNODATA         13
#define TNODIS          14
#define TNOUDERR        15
#define TBADFLAG        16
#define TNOREL          17
#define TNOTSUPPORT     18
#define TSTATECHNG      19
```

Figure 6-57: `<sys/tiuser.h>`, **Event Bitmasks**

```
#define T_LISTEN        0x0001
#define T_CONNECT       0x0002
#define T_DATA          0x0004
#define T_EXDATA        0x0008
#define T_DISCONNECT    0x0010
#define T_ERROR         0x0020
#define T_UDERR         0x0040
#define T_ORDREL        0x0080
#define T_EVENTS        0x00ff
```

Figure 6-58: `<sys/tiuser.h>`, **Flags**

```
#define T_MORE          0x001
#define T_EXPEDITED     0x002
#define T_NEGOTIATE     0x004
#define T_CHECK         0x008
#define T_DEFAULT       0x010
#define T_SUCCESS       0x020
#define T_FAILURE       0x040
```

Figure 6-59: `<sys/tiuser.h>`, **Service Types**

```
#define T_COTS          01
#define T_COTS_ORD      02
#define T_CLTS          03
```

Figure 6-60: <sys/tiuser.h>, Transport Interface Data Structures, 1 of 2

```
struct t_info {
        long                    addr;
        long                    options;
        long                    tsdu;
        long                    etsdu;
        long                    connect;
        long                    discon;
        long                    servtype;
};

struct netbuf {
        unsigned int            maxlen;
        unsigned int            len;
        char                    *buf;
};

struct t_bind {
        struct netbuf           addr;
        unsigned                qlen;
};

struct t_optmgmt {
        struct netbuf           opt;
        long                    flags;
};
```

Figure 6-61: `<sys/tiuser.h>`, Transport Interface Data Structures, 2 of 2

```
struct t_discon {
        struct netbuf           udata;
        int                     reason;
        int                     sequence;
};

struct t_call {
        struct netbuf           addr;
        struct netbuf           opt;
        struct netbuf           udata;
        int                     sequence;
};

struct t_unitdata {
        struct netbuf           addr;
        struct netbuf           opt;
        struct netbuf           udata;
};

struct t_uderr {
        struct netbuf           addr;
        struct netbuf           opt;
        long                    error;
};
```

Figure 6-62: `<sys/tiuser.h>`, **Structure Types**

```
#define T_BIND          1
#define T_OPTMGMT       2
#define T_CALL          3
#define T_DIS           4
#define T_UNITDATA      5
#define T_UDERROR       6
#define T_INFO          7
```

Figure 6-63: `<sys/tiuser.h>`, **Fields of Structures**

```
#define T_ADDR          0x01
#define T_OPT           0x02
#define T_UDATA         0x04
#define T_ALL           0x07
```


INTEL386™ FAMILY BCS

Figure 6-64: `<sys/tiuser.h>`, **Transport Interface States**

```
#define T_UNINIT        0
#define T_UNBND         1
#define T_IDLE          2
#define T_OUTCON        3
#define T_INCON         4
#define T_DATAXFER      5
#define T_OUTREL        6
#define T_INREL         7
#define T_FAKE          8
#define T_NOSTATES      9
```

Figure 6-65: `<sys/tiuser.h>`, **User-level Events**

```
#define T_OPEN          0
#define T_BIND          1
#define T_OPTMGMT       2
#define T_UNBIND        3
#define T_CLOSE         4
#define T_SNDUDATA      5
#define T_RCVUDATA      6
#define T_RCVUDERR      7
#define T_CONNECT1      8
#define T_CONNECT2      9
#define T_RCVCONNECT    10
#define T_LISTN         11
#define T_ACCEPT1       12
#define T_ACCEPT2       13
#define T_ACCEPT3       14
#define T_SND           15
#define T_RCV           16
#define T_SNDDIS1       17
#define T_SNDDIS2       18
#define T_RCVDIS1       19
#define T_RCVDIS2       20
#define T_RCVDIS3       21
#define T_SNDREL        22
#define T_RCVREL        23
#define T_PASSCON       24
#define T_NOEVENTS      25
```

Figure 6-66: `<sys/types.h>`

```
typedef unsigned char       uchar_t;
typedef unsigned long       ulong_t;

typedef char *              caddr_t;
typedef long                daddr_t;
typedef long                off_t;
typedef long                key_t;
typedef unsigned short      uid_t;
typedef unsigned short      gid_t;
typedef short               nlink_t;
typedef short               dev_t;
typedef ushort              ino_t;
typedef unsigned int        size_t;
typedef long                time_t;
typedef long                clock_t;

typedef unsigned short      ushort;
typedef unsigned long       ulong;

typedef unsigned char       u_char;
typedef unsigned short      u_short;
typedef unsigned int        u_int;
typedef unsigned long       u_long;
```

Figure 6-67: `<unistd.h>`, **Part 1 of 2**

```
#define R_OK                    4
#define W_OK                    2
#define X_OK                    1
#define F_OK                    0

#define F_ULOCK                 0
#define F_LOCK                  1
#define F_TLOCK                 2
#define F_TEST                  3

#define SEEK_SET                0
#define SEEK_CUR                1
#define SEEK_END                2

#define _SC_ARG_MAX             0
#define _SC_CHILD_MAX           1
#define _SC_CLK_TCK             2
#define _SC_NGROUPS_MAX         3
#define _SC_OPEN_MAX            4
#define _SC_JOB_CONTROL         5
#define _SC_SAVED_IDS           6
#define _SC_VERSION             7
```

Figure 6-68: `<unistd.h>`, **Part 2 of 2**

```
#define  _PC_LINK_MAX             0
#define  _PC_MAX_CANON            1
#define  _PC_MAX_INPUT            2
#define  _PC_NAME_MAX             3
#define  _PC_PATH_MAX             4
#define  _PC_PIPE_BUF             5
#define  _PC_CHOWN_RESTRICTED     6
#define  _PC_NO_TRUNC             7
#define  _PC_VDISABLE             8

#define  STDIN_FILENO             0
#define  STDOUT_FILENO            1
#define  STDERR_FILENO            2
```

Figure 6-69: `<sys/utsname.h>`

```
struct utsname {
        char    sysname[9];
        char    nodename[9];
        char    release[9];
        char    version[9];
        char    machine[9];
};
```

Figure 6-70: <wait.h>

```
#define WUNTRACED             0002
#define WNOHANG               0001

#define WIFEXITED(stat)       ((stat&0xff)==0)
#define WIFSIGNALED(stat)     ((stat)&&(stat==(stat&0x00ff)))
#define WIFSTOPPED(stat)      ((stat&0xff)==0x7f)

#define WEXITSTATUS(stat)     ((stat>>8)&0xff)
#define WTERMSIG(stat)        (stat&0x7f)
#define WSTOPSIG(stat)        ((stat>>8)&0xff)
```

7   SYSTEM FILE FORMATS

Introduction	7-1
Archive File	7-2
Future Directions	7-6
Other Archive Formats	7-7
Group File	7-8
Future Directions	7-8
Terminfo Data Base	7-9
Utmp File	7-12
Future Directions	7-14

Introduction

This chapter describes file formats that are visible to applications or that must be portable across iBCS implementations. Although the system provides standard programs to manipulate files in the formats described here, portability is important enough to warrant descriptions of their formats.

This does not mean applications are encouraged to circumvent the system programs and manipulate the files directly. Instead, it means a iBCS-conforming system must provide the system programs for manipulating these file formats. Moreover, those programs must accept formats compatible with the ones described here.

Programs that depend on undocumented formats — or that depend on the existence of undocumented files — are not iBCS-conforming. Some file formats, such as the password file in **/etc/passwd**, are defined in other standards documents. These definitions therefore do not appear in the iBCS, because the iBCS does not replicate information available in other documents. Nonetheless, an iBCS-conforming program may use the files when the file names and formats are defined implicitly for the iBCS through references to other documents.

Archive File

Archives package multiple files into one. They are commonly used as libraries
of relocatable object files to be searched by the link editor [see ld(SD_CMD)].
An archive file has the following format:

- An archive magic string, ARMAG below;

- An optional archive symbol table (created only if at least one member is
  an object file that defines non-local symbols);

- An optional archive string table (created only if at least one archive
  member's name is more than 15 bytes long);

- For each "object" file in the archive, an archive header and the unchanged
  contents of the file.

The archive file's magic string contains SARMAG bytes and does *not* include a terminating null byte.

Figure 7-1 shows the format of the archive header.

Figure 7-1: <ar.h>

```
#define ARMAG          "!<arch>\n"
#define SARMAG         8
#define ARFMAG         "'\n"


struct ar_hdr {
        char    ar_name[16];
        char    ar_date[12];
        char    ar_uid[6];
        char    ar_gid[6];
        char    ar_mode[8];
        char    ar_size[10];
        char    ar_fmag[2];
};
```

All information in the member headers is printable ASCII.

ar_name
This field represents the member's file name. If the name fits, it resides in this field directly, terminated with slash (/) and padded with blanks on the right. If the member's name is too long to fit, this field contains a slash, followed by the decimal representation of the name's offset in the archive string table.

ar_date
This field holds the decimal representation of the modification date of the file at the time of its insertion into the archive. stat(BA_OS) and time(BA_OS) describe the modification time value.

ar_uid
This field holds the decimal representation of the member's user identification number.

ar_gid
This field holds the decimal representation of the member's group identification number.

ar_mode
This field holds the octal representation of the file system mode.

ar_size
This field holds the decimal representation of the member's size in bytes.

ar_fmag
This field holds the first two bytes of the ARFMAG string, defined above.

Each member begins on an even byte boundary; a newline is inserted between files if necessary. Nevertheless the ar_size field reflects the actual size of the member exclusive of padding. There is no provision for empty areas in an archive file.

If some archive member's name is more than 15 bytes long, a special archive member will contain a table of file names, each followed by a slash and a newline. Although this string table member must precede any member with a long name, its position in the archive may vary.

Offset	+0	+1	+2	+3	+4	+5	+6	+7	+8	+9
0	f	i	l	e	n	a	m	e	s	a
10	m	p	l	e	/	\n	l	o	n	g
20	e	r	f	i	l	e	n	a	m	e
30	x	a	m	p	l	e	/	\n		

The `ar_name` entry of the string table's member header holds a zero length name (`ar_name[0]=='/'`), followed by one trailing slash (`ar_name[1]=='/'`), followed by blanks (`ar_name[2]==' '`, etc.). Offsets into the string table begin at zero. Example `ar_name` values for short and long file names appear in Figure 7-2.

Figure 7-2: Example String Table

Member Name	ar_name	Note
short-name	short-name/	Not in string table
filenamesample	/0	Offset 0 in string table
longerfilenamexample	/16	Offset 16 in string table

If an archive file has one or more object file members, its first member must be an archive symbol table. This archive member has a zero length name, followed by blanks (`ar_name[0]=='/'`, `ar_name[1]==' '`, etc.). All *words* in this symbol table have four bytes, using the machine-independent encoding shown in Figure 7-3.

NOTE: All machines use the encoding described here for the symbol table, even if the machine's "natural" byte order is different.

Figure 7-3: Archive Word Encoding

| 0x01020304 | 0 01 | 1 02 | 2 03 | 3 04 |

The symbol table holds the following:

- A word containing the number of symbols in the symbol table (which is the same as the number of entries in the file offset array);

- An array of words, holding file offsets into the archive;

- The string table containing `ar_size-4*`(*number symbols+1*) bytes, whose initial byte is numbered 0 and whose last byte holds a 0 value.

Entries in the string table and in the file offset array exactly correspond to each other, and they both parallel the order of archive members. Thus if two or more archive members define symbols with the same name (which is allowed), their string table entries will appear in the same order as their corresponding members in the archive file. Each array entry associates a symbol with the archive member that defines the symbol; the file offset is the location of the archive header for the designated archive member.

As an example, the symbol table in Figure 7-4 defines 4 symbols. The archive member at file offset 114 defines `name` and `object`. The archive member at file offset 426 defines `function` and a second version of `name`.

Figure 7-4: Example Symbol Table

Offset	+0	+1	+2	+3	
0	4				4 offset entries
4	114				name
8	114				object
12	426				function
16	426				name
20	n	a	m	e	
24	\0	o	b	j	
28	e	c	t	\0	
32	f	u	n	c	
36	t	i	o	n	
40	\0	n	a	m	
44	e	\0			

Future Directions

Currently, archive member names are limited to 15 bytes plus a terminating
slash character. A future version of the file format will allow longer member
names.

Other Archive Formats

iBCS-conforming systems support archives created by the cpio(BU_CMD) command. These archives are commonly used as a vehicle for collecting ASCII files for storage or transmission.

More information about these archives is included in the **SVID** page for cpio(BU_CMD). The format of the archives the command creates is included in the IEEE **POSIX P1003.1** specification.

Group File

This section on group file format is at Level 2.

Library routines described in getgrent(SD_LIB) provide access to the group file in /etc/group. The group file contains the following information for each group.

1. group name

2. encrypted password

3. numerical group ID

4. list of all users allowed in the group, separated by commas (,)

This is an ASCII file. The fields are separated by colons (:); each group is separated from the next by a new-line.

Future Directions

Although the file format itself is marked as Level 2, the routines to manipulate the group file will continue to exist. A future version of the system will make the true file format invisible to application programs.

Terminfo Data Base

Each terminal's capabilities are stored in a separate file named /usr/lib/terminfo/L/terminal_name, where terminal_name is the name of the terminal, and L is the first letter of the terminal's name. The specific capabilities described in the database and their names are given in the SVID on the terminfo(TI_ENV) pages. The format of this file is given in the following sections.

The terminfo database format is hardware-independent. An 8-bit byte is assumed. Short integers are stored in two contiguous 8-bit bytes. The first byte contains the least significant 8 bits of the value, and the second byte contains the most significant 8 bits. (Thus, the value represented is 256*second+first.) The value −1 is represented by 0377, 0377, and the value −2 is represented by 0376, 0377; other negative values are illegal. Computers where this does not correspond to the hardware read the integers as two bytes and compute the result, making the compiled entries portable across machine types. A −1 or a −2 in a capability field means that the capability is missing from a terminal.

The file contains six sections:

header
: The header contains six short integers in the following format: (1) the magic number (octal 0432); (2) the size, in bytes, of the names section; (3) the number of bytes in the boolean section; (4) the number of short integers in the numbers section; (5) the number of offsets (short integers) in the strings section; (6) the size, in bytes, of the string table.

terminal names
: The terminal names section contains the first line of the terminfo(TI_ENV) description, listing the various names for the terminal, separated by the '|' character. The section is terminated with an ASCII NUL character.

boolean flags
: The boolean flags indicate the terminal's capabilities. There is one byte for each flag. This byte is either 0 or 1 to indicate whether a capability is present or absent. The terminal capabilities are stored here in the same order in which they are listed under the Booleans heading of the capability table in the terminfo(TI_ENV) section of the SVID. A flag value of 2 means that the flag is invalid.

Between the boolean section and the number section, a null byte will be inserted, if necessary, to insure that the number section begins on a byte with an even-numbered address. All short integers are aligned on a short word boundary.

numbers

The numbers section is similar to the preceding boolean flags section in that it lists terminal capabilities. Each capability is stored in two bytes as a short integer. Terminal capabilities are stored here in the same order in which they are listed under the **Numbers** heading of the capability table in the `terminfo(TI_ENV)` section of the **SVID**. If the value represented is −1 or −2, the capability is missing.

strings

In the strings section, each capability is stored as a short integer, in the format given above. Terminal capabilities are stored here in the same order in which they are listed under the **Strings** heading of the capability table in the `terminfo(TI_ENV)` section of the **SVID**. A value of −1 or −2 means that a capability is missing. Otherwise, the value is taken as an offset from the beginning of the string table. Special characters in ^X or \c notation are stored in their interpreted form, not the printing representation. Padding information ($<nn>) and parameter information (%x) are stored intact in uninterpreted form.

string table

The string table contains all the values of string capabilities referenced in the string section. Again, each capability is stored as a short integer, in the format given above. Terminal capabilities are stored here in the same order in which they are listed under the **Strings** heading of the capability table in the `terminfo(TI_ENV)` section of the **SVID**. Each string is null terminated.

As an example, an octal dump of the compiled description for an AT&T Model 37 KSR is shown in Figure 7-5:

Figure 7-5: Example Dump of a Compiled Description

```
37|tty37|AT&T model 37 teletype,
    hc, os, xon,
    bel=^G, cr=\r, cub1=\b, cud1=\n, cuu1=\E7, hd=\E9,
    hu=\E8, ind=\n,

0000000 032 001       \0 032  \0 013  \0 021 001   3  \0   3   7   |   t
0000020   t   y   3   7   |   A   T   &   T       m   o   d   e   l
0000040   3   7       t   e   l   e   t   y   p   e  \0  \0  \0  \0  \0
0000060  \0  \0  \0 001  \0  \0  \0  \0  \0  \0  \0 001  \0  \0  \0  \0
0000100 001  \0  \0  \0  \0  \0 377 377 377 377 377 377 377 377 377 377
0000120 377 377 377 377 377 377 377 377 377 377 377 377 377 377   &  \0
0000140      \0 377 377 377 377 377 377 377 377 377 377 377 377 377 377
0000160 377 377   "  \0 377 377 377 377   (  \0 377 377 377 377 377 377
0000200 377 377   0  \0 377 377 377 377 377 377 377 377   -  \0 377 377
0000220 377 377 377 377 377 377 377 377 377 377 377 377 377 377 377 377
*
0000520 377 377 377 377 377 377 377 377 377 377 377 377 377 377   $  \0
0000540 377 377 377 377 377 377 377 377 377 377 377 377 377 377   *  \0
0000560 377 377 377 377 377 377 377 377 377 377 377 377 377 377 377 377
*
0001160 377 377 377 377 377 377 377 377 377 377 377 377 377 377   3   7
0001200   |   t   t   y   3   7   |   A   T   &   T       m   o   d   e
0001220   1       3   7       t   e   l   e   t   y   p   e  \0  \r  \0
0001240  \n  \0  \n  \0 007  \0  \b  \0 033   8  \0 033   9  \0 033   7
0001260  \0  \0
0001261
```

Some limitations of the terminfo database are: total compiled entries cannot
exceed 4096 bytes and all entries in the name field cannot exceed 128 bytes.

Utmp File

This section on utmp file format is at Level 2.

The utmp file in /etc/utmp contains system accounting information. Library routines described in getut(SD_LIB) provides access to the files. The file format appears in Figure 7-6.

Figure 7-6: Utmp File Format

```
struct utmp {
        char            ut_user[8];
        char            ut_id[4];
        char            ut_line[12];
        short           ut_pid;
        short           ut_type;
        struct exit_status {
            short                   e_termination;
            short                   e_exit;
        } ut_exit;
        time_t          ut_time;
};

#define EMPTY             0
#define RUN_LVL           1
#define BOOT_TIME         2
#define OLD_TIME          3
#define NEW_TIME          4
#define INIT_PROCESS      5
#define LOGIN_PROCESS     6
#define USER_PROCESS      7
#define DEAD_PROCESS      8
#define ACCOUNTING        9
```

Future Directions

Although the file format itself is marked as level 2, the routines to manipulate the utmp file will continue to exist. A future version of the system will make the true file format invisible to application programs.

Commands for Application Programs 8-1

Commands for Application Programs

Programs running on iBCS-conforming systems may create new processes and execute programs provided by the system. They can also execute a shell in a new process, and then use that shell to interpret a script that causes many system programs to be executed.

The system commands listed below must be available to applications executing on an iBCS-conforming system. They include commands from the **SVID** Basic and Advanced Utilities Extensions. For detailed information about the syntax and semantics of each command, see the appropriate **SVID** manual page.

The following commands must be available to application programs running on iBCS-conforming systems:

```
cat       expr      pg        test *
cd *      false     pr        touch
chgrp     find      pwd       tr
chmod     grep      rm        true
chown     id        rmdir     tty
cmp       kill      sed       umask *
cp        line      sh        uname
cpio      ln        sleep     uucp
date      logname   sort      uulog
dd        lp        stty      uustat
df        ls        su        uux
echo *    mkdir     tail      vi
ed        mv        tar       wait *
ex        passwd    tee       who
```

Commands marked with an asterisk above may be built into the standard UNIX System shell (/bin/sh).

9 EXECUTION ENVIRONMENT

Application Environment   9-1

File System Structure and Contents   9-3
Required Commands   9-3
Required Directories and Data Files   9-3
Required Device Files   9-4
Optional Device Files   9-5

Console Device Control   9-8
Display Escape Sequences   9-8
Console Ioctls   9-10
- Console Keyboard Ioctls   9-11
- Console Display Adapter/Virtual Terminal Ioctls   9-13
- Reserved Ioctl Values   9-17

Application Environment

This section specifies the execution environment information available to application programs running on iBCS-conforming computers. It also specifies the program interface to that information.

The execution environment contains certain information that is provided by the operating system and is available to executing application programs. Generally speaking, this includes system-wide environment information and per-process information that is accessible only to the single process to which it applies. This environment information and the utilities used to retrieve it are specified in detail in the **SVID**.

The environment information available to application programs on an iBCS-conforming system includes the following:

- System identification

  Application programs may obtain system identification information through the uname(BA_OS) system call or the system command uname(BU_CMD).

- Date and time

  The current calendar date and time are available to application programs through the date(BU_CMD) system command and the time(BA_OS) system call.

- Numerical Limits

  This refers to the maximum and minimum values of operating system variables and C language limits that application programs require. These system values are defined in the Data Definition section in Chapter 6 of the iBCS. Other system parameters are accessible through the ulimit(BA_OS) system call.

- Per-process environment information

  When an application program first begins execution an environment is made available to it. The **SVID** pages for envvar(BA_ENV), exec(BA_OS), and system(BA_OS) contain detailed descriptions of this information.

The **SVID** is the definitive reference for information about the execution environment of UNIX processes; all of this information applies to iBCS-conforming systems. The specific **SVID** references given above will lead an interested reader to all appropriate information, but are not exhaustive in themselves.

File System Structure and Contents

The file system on an iBCS-conforming system is a tree-like structure. It must contain the files and directories explicitly noted in this section. iBCS-conforming applications should make no assumptions about the file system other than relying on those file system features explicitly described in this section.

This section lists the directories and system data files that must be present on a conforming system. It also includes the format specifications of the required data files.

Required Commands

/bin/sh   This file contains the executable image of the UNIX System shell. This utility is required for the implementation of the system() function.

Required Directories and Data Files

/tmp
/usr/tmp   These directories are provided as locations to create temporary working files. These directories are the only place where applications may create such files.

/dev   This directory contains entries for all device-type file tree entries on the system.

/bin   This directory contains system utility programs required for system initialization.

/usr/bin   This directory contains system utility programs.

/opt   This directory is for the installation of static application software. See the Software Installation chapter of this specification for more information.

/opt/bin   This directory holds executable files installed by application software. See the Software Installation chapter of this specification for more information.

/var/opt	This directory holds data files created by applications, such as log files and spool files. See the Software Installation chapter of this specification for more information.
/etc	This directory contains system data files that are useful for application programs.
/etc/opt	This directory contains machine-specific configuration files installed by applications. See the Software Installation chapter of this specification for more information.
/etc/group	This system data file contains information required to implement several library functions. The file consists of ASCII characters, and is readable by all processes. Its format is described in Chapter 7, **System File Formats**. This file contains information necessary to implement several library functions. The file consists of ASCII characters, and is readable by all processes. The format of this file is given in the **SVID**, on the passwd(BA_ENV) page.
/etc/utmp	This file contains data that is used by several library functions and is readable by all processes. The format of this file is described in Chapter 7, **System File Formats**.
/usr/lib/terminfo	This directory is the top of a subtree that contains a library of capabilities for different terminals. The structure of this subtree and each of the files it contains is described in Chapter 7, **System File Formats**.

Required Device Files

/dev/null	This device file is a special "null" device that may be used to test programs or provide a data sink. This file is writable by all processes.
/dev/tty	This device file is a special one that directs all output to the controlling TTY of the current process group. This file is readable and writable by all processes.

`/dev/console`

This device file represents the system console. Output sent to this file is printed on the system console. Normally applications should not use this device to communicate with the user, but should use the `/dev/tty` device or the stdin, stdout, and stderr streams.

Optional Device Files

 **NOTE** THE FACILITIES AND INTERFACES DESCRIBED IN THIS SECTION ARE OPTIONAL COMPONENTS OF the Intel386 Family Binary Compatibility Specification.

`/dev/ttyXX`
`/dev/sxtXXX`
`/dev/xtXXX`

These device files, where **XX** represents a two-digit integer, represent device entries for terminal sessions. All these device files must be examined by the `ttyname()` call. Applications must not have the device names `/dev/ttyXX` hard-coded within them. The **xt** and **sxt** entries are optional in the system but, if present, they must be included in the library routine's search.

`/dev/cga`
`/dev/color`
`/dev/colour`

These device files are used to control the CGA graphics controller, if one is available on the system.

`/dev/ega`

This device file is used to control the EGA graphics controller, if one is available on the system.

`/dev/vga`

This device file is used to control the VGA graphics controller, if one is available on the system.

The floppy disk device names shown in Figure 9-1 will exist as described, if the corresponding floppy disk device is available on the system.

Figure 9-1: Floppy Disk Device Names

Name	Device
/dev/[r]fd[01]	"Default" density drive (/etc/default/format)
/dev/[r]fd[01]48ds9	5.25" 360 KB, (48 tpi, 2 sided, 9 spt)
/dev/[r]fd[01]96ds15	5.25" 1.2 MB, (96 tpi, 2 sided, 15 spt)
/dev/[r]fd[01]96	5.25" 1.2 MB, (96 tpi, 2 sided, 15 spt)
/dev/[r]fd[01]135ds9	3.5" 720 KB, (135 tpi, 2 sided, 9 spt)
/dev/[r]fd[01]135ds18	3.5" 1.44 MB, (135 tpi, 2 sided, 18 spt)
/dev/[r]dsk/f[01][t]	Automatic format detection
/dev/[r]dsk/f[01]3d[t]	3.5" 720 KB, (135 tpi, 2 sided, 9 spt)
/dev/[r]dsk/f[01]3h[t]	3.5" 1.44 MB, (135 tpi, 2 sided, 18 spt)
/dev/[r]dsk/f[01]5d9[t]	5.25" 360 KB, (48 tpi, 2 sided, 9 spt)
/dev/[r]dsk/f[01]5h[t]	5.25" 1.2 MB, (96 tpi, 2 sided, 15 spt)
/dev/[r]dsk/f[01]d9d[t]	Link to /dev/[r]dsk/f[01]5d9[t]
/dev/[r]dsk/f[01]q15d[t]	Link to /dev/[r]dsk/f[01]5h[t]
/dev/install	Drive 0 automatic format detection
/dev/install1	Drive 1 automatic format detection
/dev/sctfdl128	Link to /dev/dsk/f05d9
/dev/sctfdl129	Link to /dev/dsk/f15d9
/dev/sctfdm0	Link to /dev/fd096
/dev/sctfdm1	Link to /dev/fd196
/dev/sctfdm128	Link to /dev/dsk/f05h
/dev/sctfdm129	Link to /dev/dsk/f15h

The 't' suffix on the /dev/[r]dsk floppy device names is used to specify the whole floppy disk. Without the 't' suffix, cylinder 0 of the floppy disk is ignored and is not read or written.

The cartridge tape device names shown in Figure 9-2 will exist as described, if the corresponding cartridge tape device is available on the system.

Figure 9-2: Cartridge Tape Device Names

Name	Device
/dev/[n]rStp0	SCSI tape unit 0 (raw device)
/dev/xStp0	SCSI tape unit 0 control device (for *ioctl(2)* processing)
/dev/rct0	QIC-24 tape unit 0 (raw device)
/dev/nrct0	QIC-24 tape unit 0 (raw device, no rewind)
/dev/xct0	Control device
/dev/rmt/c0s[01][n][r]	QIC-24 tape unit

The 'n' suffix on the /dev/rmt cartridge tape device names is used to specify no rewind when the device is closed. Without the 'n' suffix, the tape is automatically rewound when the device is closed. The 'r' suffix on the /dev/rmt cartridge tape device names is used to specify no retension when the device is opened. Without the 'r' suffix, the tape is automatically retensioned when the device is opened.

Console Device Control

NOTE THE FACILITIES AND INTERFACES DESCRIBED IN THIS SECTION ARE OPTIONAL COMPONENTS OF the **Intel386 Family Binary Compatibility Specification.**

The console keyboard and display connected to the system can be controlled by a sequence of **ioctl** commands or sending a sequence of command characters to the display device. These commands used to control the console display device are optional. However, if a CGA, EGA or VGA graphics controller based console device is available, then these commands must be implemented as specified.

Display Escape Sequences

The ANSI X3.64 standard specifies two character sequences that are to be interpreted as the command sequence initiator (CSI). One is for the 7-bit character set and is equal to the character sequence "<ESC>[" while the other is for the 8-bit character set and is the character '\0233'. In Figure 9-3, the term CSI means either of the above sequence of characters.

Figure 9-3: Console Escape Sequences

Character Sequence	Meaning
CSI 0k	disable key click
CSI 1k	enable key click
CSI 2h	lock keyboard
CSI 2i	send screen as input
CSI 2l	unlock keyboard
CSI 6m	enable background color intensity
CSI <0-2>c	*reserved*
CSI <0-59>m	select graphic rendition
CSI <$n;m$>H	cursor to line n and column m
CSI <$n;m$>f	cursor to line n and column m
CSI <n>@	insert character(s)
CSI <n>A	cursor up n lines
CSI <n>B	cursor down n lines
CSI <n>C	cursor right n characters
CSI <n>D	cursor left n characters
CSI <n>E	cursor down n lines and in first column
CSI <n>F	cursor up n lines and in first column
CSI <n>G	position cursor at column n-1
CSI <n>J	erase in display
CSI <n>K	erase in line
CSI <n>L	insert line(s)
CSI <n>M	delete line(s)
CSI <n>P	delete character(s)
CSI <n>S	scroll up n lines
CSI <n>T	scroll down n lines
CSI <n>X	erase characters
CSI <n>Z	back cursor up n tab stops
CSI <n>'	cursor to column n on line
CSI <n>a	cursor right n characters
CSI <n>d	cursor to line n
CSI <n>e	cursor down n lines
CSI <n>g	clear tab stops
CSI <n>z	make virtual terminal number n active
CSI ?7h	turn automargin on
CSI ?7l	turn automargin off
CSI s †	save cursor position

Figure 9-3: Console Escape Sequences (continued)

CSI u †	restore cursor position to saved value
CSI=<c>A	set overscan color
CSI=<c>F	set normal foreground color
CSI=<c>G	set normal background color
CSI=<c>H	set reverse foreground color
CSI=<c>I	set reverse background color
CSI=<c>J	set graphic foreground color
CSI=<c>K	set graphic background color
CSI=<n>g	display *n* from alternate graphics character set
CSI=<p;d>B	set bell parameters
CSI=<s;e>C	set cursor parameters
CSI=<x>D	enable/disable intensity of background color
CSI=<x>E	set/clear blink vs. bold background
ESC 7	save cursor position
ESC 8	restore cursor position to saved value
ESC H	set tab stop
ESC Q<n><delim>*<string>*<delim>	define function key string
ESC c	clear display

The console escape sequences marked with "†" in Figure 9-3 are at Level 2.

Console Ioctls

ioctl values are used to control the console keyboard and display adapter or virtual terminal. Values for **ioctls** are formed by OR'ing a command number with an **ioctl** type, where the command is the least significant byte of the **ioctl** value and the type is the remaining significant bytes. Typically, the type is a one-byte value itself, so that the **ioctl** value will fit in a 2-byte quantity. However, that need not always be the case.

Figure 9-4 shows the **ioctl** type definitions.

Figure 9-4: ioctl Type Definitions

NAME	VALUE
KIOC	('K'<<8)
MIOC	('k'<<8)
MAPADAPTER	('m'<<8)
SWAPCONS	('s'<<8)
PGAIOC	('P'<<8)
CGAIOC	('C'<<8)
MCAIOC	('M'<<8)
EGAIOC	('E'<<8)
VGAIOC	('E'<<8)
TIOC	('T'<<8)
VTIOC	('v'<<8)
CONSIOC	('c'<<8)
WSIOC	(('w'<<24)|('s'<<16))
EVGAIOC	(('E'<<24)|('V'<<16))
MODESWITCH	(('i'<<24)|('x'<<16))
C_IOC	(('i'<<24)|('C'<<16))
XIOC	(('i'<<24)|('X'<<16))

The WSIOC and EVGAIOC types are reserved and should not be used by iBCS-conforming programs, they are shown only for completeness.

Console Keyboard Ioctls

Figure 9-5 lists the symbolic names and values for **ioctls** that can be used to control the console keyboard.

Figure 9-5: Console Keyboard Ioctls

NAME	VALUE	DESCRIPTION
KDGKBMODE	(KIOC|6)	Get keyboard translation mode
KDSKBMODE	(KIOC|7)	Set keyboard translation mode
KDGKBSTATE	(KIOC|19)	Get state of keyboard shift keys
KIOCINFO	(KIOC|62)	Determine workstation of VT
KIOCSOUND	(KIOC|63)	Start sound generation
KDGKBTYPE	(KIOC|64)	Get keyboard type
KDGETLED	(KIOC|65)	Get keyboard LED status
KDSETLED	(KIOC|66)	Set keyboard LED status
GETFKEY	(MIOC|0)	Get function key
SETFKEY	(MIOC|1)	Set function key
GIO_STRMAP	(MIOC|11)	Get function key string table
PIO_STRMAP	(MIOC|12)	Set function key string table
TIOCKBON	(TIOC|8)	Turn on extended keys
TIOCKBOF	(TIOC|9)	Turn off extended keys
KBENABLED	(TIOC|10)	Are extended keys enabled?

The console keyboard ioctls in Figure 9-6 are at Level 2.

Figure 9-6: Level 2 Console Keyboard Ioctls

NAME	VALUE	DESCRIPTION
GIO_STRMAP_21	(MIOC|4)	Get 2.1 function key string table
PIO_STRMAP_21	(MIOC|5)	Put 2.1 function key string table
GIO_KEYMAP	(MIOC|6)	Get the keyboard map table
PIO_KEYMAP	(MIOC|7)	Put the keyboard map table
SETLOCKLOCK	(MIOC|10)	Global cap/num lock on/off
KBIO_SETMODE	(MIOC|13)	Set the AT/XT keyboard mode
KBIO_GETMODE	(MIOC|14)	Get the AT/XT keyboard mode

Console Display Adapter/Virtual Terminal Ioctls

Figure 9-7 lists the symbolic names and values for **ioctls** that can be used to control the console display adapter or the console virtual terminal.

Figure 9-7: Console Display Adapter/Virtual Terminal Ioctls

NAME	VALUE	DESCRIPTION
KDDISPTYPE	(KIOC|1)	Return display type to user
KDMAPDISP	(KIOC|2)	Map display into user space
KDUNMAPDISP	(KIOC|3)	Unmap display from user space
KDGETMODE	(KIOC|9)	Get text/graphics mode
KDSETMODE	(KIOC|10)	Set text/graphics mode
KDSBORDER	(KIOC|13)	Set EGA color border
KDDISPINFO	(KIOC|18)	Get display start and size
KDENABIO	(KIOC|60)	Enable direct I/O to ports
KDDISABIO	(KIOC|61)	Disable direct I/O to ports
GIO_SCRNMAP	(MIOC|2)	Get screen output map table
GIO_ATTR	('a'<<8)	Get present screen attribute
GIO_COLOR	('c'<<8)	Get whether adaptor is color
CONS_CURRENT	(CONSIOC|1)	Get display adapter type
CONS_GET	(CONSIOC|2)	Get display mode setting
CONSIO	(CONSIOC|3)	Do inb/outb on console port
CONS_BLANKTIME	(CONSIOC|4)	Set time before inactive screen blanked
PIO_FONT8x8	(CONSIOC|64)	Use user-supplied 8x8 font
GIO_FONT8x8	(CONSIOC|65)	Get current 8x8 font in use

Figure 9-7: Console Display Adapter/Virtual Terminal Ioctls (continued)

PIO_FONT8x14	(CONSIOC|66)	Use user-supplied 8x14 font
GIO_FONT8x14	(CONSIOC|67)	Get current 8x14 font in use
PIO_FONT8x16	(CONSIOC|68)	Use user-supplied 8x16 font
GIO_FONT8x16	(CONSIOC|69)	Get current 8x16 font in use
CONSADP	(CONSIOC|72)	Get active VT number
CONS_GETINFO	(CONSIOC|73)	Get vid_info struct
CONS_6845INFO	(CONSIOC|74)	Get m6845_info struct
VT_SETMODE	(VTIOC|2)	Set VT into auto or process mode
VT_GETMODE	(VTIOC|3)	Returns mode VT is currently in
VT_RELDISP	(VTIOC|4)	Tells VT when display released
VT_ACTIVATE	(VTIOC|5)	Activates specified VT
SW_B40x25	(MODESWITCH|0)	Select 40x25 b&w
SW_C40x25	(MODESWITCH|1)	Select 40x25 color
SW_B80x25	(MODESWITCH|2)	Select 80x25 b&w
SW_C80x25	(MODESWITCH|3)	Select 80x25 color
SW_BG320	(MODESWITCH|4)	Select 320x200 b&w
SW_CG320	(MODESWITCH|5)	Select 320x200 color
SW_BG640	(MODESWITCH|6)	Select 640x200 b&w
SW_EGAMONO80x25	(MODESWITCH|7)	Select EGA mode 7
SW_CG320_D	(MODESWITCH|13)	Select EGA mode D
SW_CG640_E	(MODESWITCH|14)	Select EGA mode E
SW_EGAMONOAPA	(MODESWITCH|15)	Select EGA mode F
SW_CG640x350	(MODESWITCH|16)	Select EGA mode 10
SW_ENH_MONOAPA2	(MODESWITCH|17)	Select EGA mode F*
SW_ENH_CG640	(MODESWITCH|18)	Select EGA mode 16
SW_ENHB40x25	(MODESWITCH|19)	Select 40x25 b&w
SW_ENHC40x25	(MODESWITCH|20)	Select 40x25 color
SW_ENHB80x25	(MODESWITCH|21)	Select 80x25 b&w
SW_ENHC80x25	(MODESWITCH|22)	Select 80x25 color
SW_ENHB80x43	(MODESWITCH|0x70)	Select 80x43 b&w
SW_ENHC80x43	(MODESWITCH|0x71)	Select 80x43 color
SW_MCAMODE	(MODESWITCH|0xff)	Reinitialize mono
SW_VGAC40x25	(MODESWITCH|23)	Select VGA 40x25 color
SW_VGAC80x25	(MODESWITCH|24)	Select VGA 80x25 color
SW_VGAMONO80x25	(MODESWITCH|25)	Select VGA mode 7
SW_VGA640x480C	(MODESWITCH|26)	Select VGA mode 11
SW_VGA640x480E	(MODESWITCH|27)	Select VGA mode 12

Figure 9-7: Console Display Adapter/Virtual Terminal Ioctls (continued)

SW_VGA320x200	(MODESWITCH|28)	Select VGA mode 13
SW_VGA40x25	SW_VGAC40x25	
SW_VGA80x25	SW_VGAC80x25	
SW_VGAM80x25	SW_VGAMONO80x25	
SW_VGA11	SW_VGA640x480C	
SW_VGA12	SW_VGA640x480E	
SW_VGA13	SW_VGA320x200	
SW_VGA_C40x25	SW_VGAC40x25	
SW_BG640x480	SW_VGA640x480C	
SW_CG640x480	SW_VGA640x480E	
SW_VGA_CG320	SW_VGA320x200	
SW_HGC_P0	(MODESWITCH|0xe0)	
SW_HGC_P1	(MODESWITCH|0xe1)	
MAP_CLASS	(C_IOC|1)	

The console display adapter/virtual terminal ioctls in Figure 9-8 are at Level 2.

Figure 9-8: Level 2 Console Display Adapter/Virtual Terminal Ioctls

NAME	VALUE	DESCRIPTION
KDADDIO	(KIOC|11)	Add I/O address to list
KDDELIO	(KIOC|12)	Delete I/O address from list
INTERNAL_VID	(CGAIOC|72)	Internal plasma monitor
EXTERNAL_VID	(CGAIOC|73)	External plasma monitor
PGAMODE	(PGAIOC|1)	Obsolete
PGAIO	(PGAIOC|2)	Do I/O on PGA port
PGA_GET	(PGAIOC|3)	Get PGA mode setting
CGAMODE	(CGAIOC|1)	Obsolete
CGAIO	(CGAIOC|2)	Do I/O on CGA port
CGA_GET	(CGAIOC|3)	Get CGA mode setting
EGAMODE	(EGAIOC|1)	Obsolete
EGAIO	(EGAIOC|2)	Do I/O on EGA port

Figure 9-8: Level 2 Console Display Adapter/Virtual Terminal Ioctls (continued)

EGA_GET	(EGAIOC|3)	Get EGA mode setting
MCAMODE	(MCAIOC|1)	Obsolete
MCAIO	(MCAIOC|2)	Do I/O on MCA port
MCA_GET	(MCAIOC|3)	Get MCA mode setting
VGAMODE	(VGAIOC|65)	Change VGA mode
VGAIO	(VGAIOC|66)	Do inb/outb on VGA port
VGA_GET	(VGAIOC|67)	Get VGA mode setting
VGA_IOPRIVL	(VGAIOC|68)	Get in/out privilege for VGA ports
EGA_IOPRIVL	(EGAIOC|4)	Get in/out privilege for EGA ports
SWAPMONO	(SWAPCONS|1)	Swap MCA adapter
SWAPCGA	(SWAPCONS|2)	Swap CGA adapter
SWAPPGA	(SWAPCONS|3)	Swap PGA adapter
SWAPEGA	(SWAPCONS|4)	Swap EGA adapter
SWAPVGA	(SWAPCONS|5)	Swap VGA adapter
MAPCONS	(MAPADAPTER)	Map display adapter memory
MAPMONO	(MAPADAPTER|1)	Map MCA adapter memory
MAPCGA	(MAPADAPTER|2)	Map CGA adapter memory
MAPPGA	(MAPADAPTER|3)	Map PGA adapter memory
MAPEGA	(MAPADAPTER|4)	Map EGA adapter memory
MAPVGA	(MAPADAPTER|5)	
O_MODESWITCH	('S'<<8)	
O_SW_B40x25	(O_MODESWITCH|0)	Select 40x25 b&w
O_SW_C40x25	(O_MODESWITCH|1)	Select 40x25 color
O_SW_B80x25	(O_MODESWITCH|2)	Select 80x25 b&w
O_SW_C80x25	(O_MODESWITCH|3)	Select 80x25 color
O_SW_BG320	(O_MODESWITCH|4)	Select 320x200 b&w
O_SW_CG320	(O_MODESWITCH|5)	Select 320x200 color
O_SW_BG640	(O_MODESWITCH|6)	Select 640x200 b&w
O_SW_EGAMONO80x25	(O_MODESWITCH|7)	Select EGA mode 7
O_SW_CG320_D	(O_MODESWITCH|13)	Select EGA mode D
O_SW_CG640_E	(O_MODESWITCH|14)	Select EGA mode E
O_SW_EGAMONOAPA	(O_MODESWITCH|15)	Select EGA mode F
O_SW_CG640x350	(O_MODESWITCH|16)	Select EGA mode 10
O_SW_ENH_MONOAPA2	(O_MODESWITCH|17)	Select EGA mode F*
O_SW_ENH_CG640	(O_MODESWITCH|18)	Select EGA mode 16
O_SW_ENHB40x25	(O_MODESWITCH|19)	Select 40x25 b&w
O_SW_ENHC40x25	(O_MODESWITCH|20)	Select 40x25 color

Figure 9-8: Level 2 Console Display Adapter/Virtual Terminal Ioctls (continued)

O_SW_ENHB80x25	(O_MODESWITCH|21)	Select 80x25 b&w
O_SW_ENHC80x25	(O_MODESWITCH|22)	Select 80x25 color
O_SW_ENHB80x43	(O_MODESWITCH|0x70)	Select 80x43 b&w
O_SW_ENHC80x43	(O_MODESWITCH|0x71)	Select 80x43 color
O_SW_MCAMODE	(O_MODESWITCH|0xff)	Reinitialize mono
O_SW_VGA40x25	(O_MODESWITCH|23)	
O_SW_VGA80x25	(O_MODESWITCH|24)	
O_SW_VGAM80x25	(O_MODESWITCH|25)	
O_SW_VGA11	(O_MODESWITCH|26)	
O_SW_VGA12	(O_MODESWITCH|27)	
O_SW_VGA13	(O_MODESWITCH|28)	
O_SW_VGA_C40x25	(O_MODESWITCH|23)	
O_SW_BG640x480	(O_MODESWITCH|26)	
O_SW_CG640x480	(O_MODESWITCH|27)	
O_SW_VGA_CG320	(O_MODESWITCH|28)	

Reserved Ioctl Values

Figure 9-9 lists the **ioctl** values that are reserved. Any program that uses these **ioctl** values are not iBCS conforming and the behavior of such programs are undefined.

Figure 9-9: Reserved Ioctl Values

NAME	VALUE	DESCRIPTION
KDGKBENT	(KIOC|4)	Get keyboard table entry
KDSKBENT	(KIOC|5)	Set keyboard table entry
KDSETRAD	(KIOC|20)	Set keyboard typematic rate/delay
MAPSPECIAL	(MAPADAPTER|100)	
KDSCROLL	(KIOC|21)	Set hardware scrolling on/off
KDQUEMODE	(KIOC|15)	Enable/disable queue mode
KIOCDOSMODE	(KIOC|16)	Obsolete — never supported
KIOCNONDOSMODE	(KIOC|17)	Obsolete — never supported
SW_VGAB40x25	(MODESWITCH|29)	Select VGA 40x25 b&w
SW_VGAB80x25	(MODESWITCH|30)	Select VGA 80x25 b&w
SW_VGAMONOAPA	(MODESWITCH|31)	Select VGA mode F+

Figure 9-9: Reserved Ioctl Values (continued)

SW_VGA_CG640	(MODESWITCH|32)	Select VGA mode 10+
SW_VGA_B40x25	SW_VGAB40x25	
SW_ATT640	(MODESWITCH|34)	Select 640x400 16 color
SW_VDC800x600E	(MODESWITCH|39)	Select 800x600 16 color
SW_VDC640x400V	(MODESWITCH|40)	Select 640x400 256 color
SW_VGA_B132x25	(MODESWITCH|35)	Select VGA 132x25 b&w
SW_VGA_C132x25	(MODESWITCH|36)	Select VGA 132x25 color
SW_VGA_B132x43	(MODESWITCH|37)	Select VGA 132x43 b&w
SW_VGA_C132x43	(MODESWITCH|38)	Select VGA 132x43 color
SW_EVC640x480V	(MODESWITCH|41)	Select 640x480 256 color
SW_EVC1024x768E	(MODESWITCH|42)	Select 1024x768 16 color
SW_EVC1024x768D	(MODESWITCH|43)	Select 1024x768 256 color
TEMPEVC1024x768E	(MODESWITCH|42)	
O_SW_ATT640	(O_MODESWITCH|34)	Select 640x400 16 color
VT_OPENQRY	(VTIOC|1)	Find number of an inactive VT
VT_WAITACTIVE	(VTIOC|6)	Wait for VT to be activated
VT_GETSTATE	(VTIOC|100)	Return active and open VTs
VT_SENDSIG	(VTIOC|101)	Send signal to specified VTs
SW_GEN_640x350	(EVGAIOC|0)	
SW_GEN_640x480	(EVGAIOC|1)	
SW_GEN_720x540	(EVGAIOC|2)	
SW_GEN_800x560	(EVGAIOC|3)	
SW_GEN_800x600	(EVGAIOC|4)	
SW_GEN_960x720	(EVGAIOC|5)	
SW_GEN_1024x768	(EVGAIOC|6)	
SW_GEN_1024x768x2	(EVGAIOC|7)	
SW_GEN_1024x768x4	(EVGAIOC|8)	
KDDFLTKEYMAP	(WSIOC|2)	Set/get default keyboard map
KDDFLTSCRNMAP	(WSIOC|3)	Set/get default screen map
KDDFLTSTRMAP	(WSIOC|4)	Set/get default function key string map
WS_PIO_ROMFONT	(WSIOC|5)	Add user-supplied font overlays
WS_CLRXXCOMPAT	(WSIOC|6)	Turn off compatibility mode on VT
WS_GETXXCOMPAT	(WSIOC|7)	Return state of compatibility mode on VT
WS_SETXXCOMPAT	(WSIOC|8)	Turn on compatibility mode on VT
KDVDCTYPE	(WSIOC|1)	VDC controller/display information
KDEVGA	(WSIOC|9)	Set EVGA card type

Index

A

address
  absolute   3: 61
  stack   3: 48
  stack object   3: 61
  unaligned   3: 5
  virtual   5: 2
addressing, virtual (see virtual
    addressing)
aggregate   3: 5
alignment
  array   3: 5
  bit-field   3: 9
  double   3: 5, 7, 25
  executable file   5: 2
  heap allocation   3: 61
  scalar types   3: 4
  stack   3: 16
  stack frame   3: 16, 59
  structure and union   3: 5
allocation
  dynamic stack space   3: 17, 57, 59
  heap space   3: 61
ANSI, C (see C language, ANSI)
architecture
  implementation   3: 3
  processor   1: 2, 3: 3, 11
archive file   7: 2
  string table   7: 2
argc   3: 44
arguments
  bad assumptions   3: 58
  exec(BA_OS)   3: 44
  floating-point   3: 24
  function   3: 14
  integer   3: 24
  main   3: 44
  order   3: 16
  pointer   3: 24
  sign extension   3: 24
  stack   3: 16, 24
  structure and union   3: 25
  variable list   3: 58
argv   3: 44
array   3: 5
ASCII   7: 3
assembler   4: 1
automatic variables   3: 57

B

base components   1: 4
BCS conformance   1: 6, 3: 3, 5, 7, 12, 25,
    31, 46, 50, 4: 2, 12, 5: 1, 6: 1, 7: 1,
    9: 17
  see also undefined behavior   3: 3
  see also unspecified property   3: 3
behavior, undefined (see undefined
    behavior)
Binary Compatibility Specification
    1: 1
/bin/sh   9: 3
bit-field   3: 8
  alignment   3: 9
  allocation   3: 9
  unnamed   3: 9
boot parameters (see tunable parame-
    ters)
bounds check fault   3: 38
branch instructions   3: 55
breakpoint trap   3: 38

C

C language
  ANSI 3: 4, 44, 58, 6: 29
  calling sequence 3: 14, 58–59
  fundamental types 3: 4
  main 3: 44
  portability 3: 58
  switch statements 3: 55
call by value 3: 25
call instruction 3: 19, 22, 52–53
calling sequence 3: 14
  function epilogue 3: 19–20, 22–23
  function prologue 3: 19, 22
cartridge tape 2: 2, 9: 7
  QIC-24 format 2: 2
char 3: 4
character sets 7: 3
code generation 3: 50
code sequences 3: 50
COFF section, object file 4: 7
COFF section header 4: 7
configuration parameters (see tunable
      parameters)
console device 9: 8
coprocessor error fault 3: 38
coprocessor overrun abort 3: 38
cpio(BU_CMD) 2: 8, 7: 7
CPU identification 3: 61
<ctype.h> 6: 30
custom software packaging 2: 26

D

data
  process 3: 27
  uninitialized 5: 3
date(BU_CMD) 9: 1

/dev/cga 9: 5
/dev/color 9: 5
/dev/colour 9: 5
/dev/console 9: 5
/dev/ega 9: 5
/dev/null 9: 4
/dev/sxtXXX 9: 5
/dev/tty 9: 4
/dev/ttyXX 9: 5
/dev/vga 9: 5
/dev/xtXXX 9: 5
<dirent.h> 6: 31
divide error fault 3: 38
double 3: 4
double fault abort 3: 38
doubleword 3: 4–5
dynamic frame size 3: 57
dynamic segments 3: 28
dynamic stack allocation 3: 59
  signals 3: 60

E

EFLAGS register, initial value 3: 44
EIP-relative 3: 55
emulation, instructions 3: 3
environment
  application 9: 1
  exec(BA_OS) 3: 44
envp 3: 44
envvar(BA_ENV) 9: 1
<errno.h> 6: 34
/etc/group 7: 8
/etc/passwd 7: 1
exceptions 3: 37
  interface 3: 37
  signals 3: 37

exec(BA_OS)   3: 46, 4: 1, 5: 4, 9: 1
  paging   5: 2
  process initialization   3: 44
executable file   4: 1
extended-precision   3: 19

F

<fcntl.h>   6: 36
file
  archive (see archive file)
  formats   7: 1
  group (see group file)
  object (see object file)
  password (see password file)
file offset   5: 2
float   3: 4
floating-point
  arguments   3: 24
  return value   3: 19
floating-point control register, initial
      value   3: 44
floating-point status register, initial
      value   3: 44
floppy disk   2: 2, 9: 6
formats
  archive file   7: 2
  array   3: 5
  file (see file)
  object file   4: 2, 12
  structure   3: 5
  union   3: 5
FORTRAN language
  COMMON   3: 5
  EQUIVALENCE   3: 5
frame pointer   3: 17
  initial value   3: 47

frame size, dynamic   3: 59
<ftw.h>   6: 37
function, void   3: 19
function arguments (see arguments)
function call, code   3: 52
function linkage (see calling
      sequence)
function prologue and epilogue (see
      calling sequence)

G

general protection fault/abort   3: 38
getgrent(SD_LIB)   7: 8
getrlimit(BA_OS)   2: 9
group file   7: 8
<grp.h>   6: 37

H

halfword   3: 4
heap
  allocation   3: 61
  dynamic stack   3: 59
heap allocation   3: 61
  alignment   3: 61

I

iBCS   1: 1, 6
<ieeefp.h>   6: 38
init(AS_CMD)   2: 9
initialization, process   3: 44
installation media   2: 2
instructions, emulation   3: 3
int   3: 4

int instruction   3: 39
integer arguments   3: 24
Intel287 coprocessor   3: 36
Intel386 processor   1: 2, 3: 3, 11, 14, 27,
      37, 58, 61, 5: 2
Intel387 coprocessor   3: 3, 5, 18–19, 36,
      38, 43, 45
Intel486 processor   1: 1, 3: 3, 11, 61
interrupt   3: 19
invalid opcode fault   3: 38
invalid TSS fault   3: 38

L

ld(SD_CMD) (see link editor)
Level 1   1: 5
Level 2   1: 5, 2: 19, 3: 30, 39, 4: 12, 6: 1,
      3, 7, 10, 7: 8, 12, 14, 9: 10, 12, 15
libc, see also library   6: 1
libnsl, see also library   6: 1
library
   see also archive file   7: 2
   see also libc   6: 1
   see also libnsl   6: 1
   see also libX11   6: 1
   shared (see shared library)
libX11, see also library   6: 1
<limits.h>   6: 41
link editor   4: 1
   ld(SD_CMD)   7: 2
linkage, function (see calling
      sequence)
local variables   3: 57
lock instruction   3: 11
long   3: 4
long double   3: 4–5
longjmp(BA_LIB) (see
      setjmp(BA_LIB))

M

Machine Status Word register, initial
      value   3: 44
magic number
   COFF   4: 3, 5
   x.out   4: 13
main
   arguments   3: 44
   declaration   3: 44
malloc(BA_OS)   3: 29, 61
<math.h>   6: 42
media format   2: 3, 19
memory, synchronization   3: 11
memory allocation
   heap   3: 61
   stack   3: 57, 59
memory management   3: 27, 5: 1
memory semaphore   3: 11

N

no coprocessor fault   3: 38
nonconforming program   1: 6
nonmaskable interrupt   3: 38
null pointer   3: 5, 28, 44

O

object file   4: 1
   archive file   7: 2
   COFF file header   4: 2
   COFF format   4: 2
   COFF section   4: 2, 7
   COFF section header   4: 2, 7
   COFF system header   4: 2, 5
   program loading   4: 7, 19, 23

see also archive file   4: 1
see also executable file   4: 1
see also shared library   4: 1
segment   5: 1–2
x.out   4: 12
x.out extended header   4: 12–13, 16
x.out format   4: 12
x.out header   4: 12–13
x.out iteration record   4: 23
x.out segment table   4: 19
x.out segments   4: 12
optimization   3: 21, 24
optional component   6: 2, 9: 8
optional components   1: 4
overflow trap   3: 38

P

P1003.1   1: 2
padding
    arguments   3: 16, 25
    structure and union   3: 6
page fault   3: 38
page size   3: 27, 5: 2
paging   3: 27, 5: 2
    performance   5: 2
parameters
    function (see arguments)
    system configuration (see tunable
        parameters)
password file   7: 1
performance, paging   5: 2
permissions, process segments (see
        segment permissions)
physical addressing   3: 27
physical format   2: 2
physical media   2: 2–3, 20

pkgadd(AS_CMD)   2: 9–10
pkgask(AS_CMD)   2: 10
pkginfo(AS_CMD)   2: 9
pointer   3: 5
    function argument   3: 24
    null   3: 5, 44
<poll.h>   6: 45
portability
    C program   3: 58
    instructions   3: 3
POSIX.1   1: 2
procedures (see functions)
process
    dead   3: 60
    entry point   3: 44, 4: 6, 14
    image   4: 1, 7, 19, 23, 5: 1
    initialization   3: 44
    segment   3: 27
    size   3: 27
    stack   3: 46
    virtual addressing   3: 27, 4: 8
processor architecture   1: 2, 3: 3, 11
processor execution mode   3: 44
processor-specific information   3: 3,
        14, 27, 50, 5: 1–2
program loading   5: 1–2
<pwd.h>   6: 45

R

re-entrancy   3: 21
register
    eax   3: 18
    ebp   3: 17
    ebx   3: 18
    ecx   3: 18
    edi   3: 18

edx 3: 18
EFLAGS 3: 18
esi 3: 18
esp 3: 17
floating-point 3: 18
floating-point control word 3: 18
floating-point return value 3: 19
register variable 3: 17–18
scratch 3: 18
register cr0 (see Machine Status
     Word register)
register eax, integer return value
     3: 19
register variables 3: 59
registers
  calling sequence 3: 17
  cs, ds, es, and ss 3: 48
  description 3: 14, 17
  floating-point 3: 14
  global 3: 14
  initial values 3: 47
relocatable file 4: 1
resources, shared 3: 27
ret instruction 3: 19, 22
return address 3: 19
return value
  floating-point 3: 19
  integer 3: 19
  pointer 3: 19
  structure and union 3: 21

S

scalar types 3: 4
<search.h> 6: 46
secondary storage 3: 27
section, object file 5: 2

segment
  dynamic 3: 28
  loadable 3: 28
  object file 5: 1
  permissions 5: 3
  process 3: 27, 5: 1–2
segment not present fault 3: 38
segment permissions 5: 1
segment registers 3: 48
setjmp(BA_LIB) 3: 60
<setjmp.h> 6: 48
shared library 4: 1
shared object file, segments 3: 28
shell scripts 4: 1
short 3: 4
sign extension
  arguments 3: 24
  bit-field 3: 9
signal(BA_OS) 3: 19, 37
<signal.h> 6: 50
signals 3: 19, 60
signed 3: 4, 8
single step trap/fault 3: 38
sizeof 3: 4
  structure 3: 6
stack
  address 3: 48
  dynamic allocation 3: 59
  growth 3: 15
  initial process 3: 47
  process 3: 27–28
  system management 3: 29
stack exception fault 3: 38
stack frame 3: 14, 16, 19, 21–22, 24, 57
  alignment 3: 16, 48, 59
  organization 3: 15–16, 56
  size 3: 17, 57
stack pointer 3: 17, 48

initial value   3: 48
stat(BA_OS)   7: 3
<stdarg.h>   3: 58
<stddef.h>   6: 53
<stdio.h>   6: 55
string table, see archive file   7: 2
<stropts.h>   6: 58
structure   3: 5
  function argument   3: 25
  padding   3: 6
  return value   3: 21
SVID   1: 1–2, 6, 2: 9, 21, 3: 31, 6: 1, 6, 9, 29, 7: 7, 9, 8: 1, 9: 1
switch statements   3: 55
synchronization, memory   3: 11
<sys/fp.h>   6: 36
<sys/ipc.h>   6: 39
<sys/lock.h>   6: 41
<sys/mount.h>   6: 42
<sys/msg.h>   6: 43
<sys/param.h>   6: 44
<sys/reg.h>   6: 46
<sys/sem.h>   6: 47
<sys/shm.h>   6: 48
<sys/statfs.h>   6: 53
<sys/stat.h>   6: 52
<sys/sysi86.h>   6: 59
system()   9: 3
system load   3: 27
System V Interface Definition, Issue 2   1: 1
system(BA_OS)   9: 1
<sys/time.h>   6: 71
<sys/times.h>   6: 72
<sys/tiuser.h>   6: 80
<sys/types.h>   6: 81
<sys/utsname.h>   6: 83

T

tar(AU_CMD)   2: 26
termination, process   3: 60
terminfo(TI_ENV)   7: 9
<termios.h>   6: 70
text, process   3: 27
time(BA_OS)   7: 3, 9: 1
tunable parameters
  process size   3: 27
  shared libraries   4: 10
type mismatch   3: 21

U

ulimit(BA_OS)   9: 1
unaligned address (see address, unaligned)
uname(BA_OS)   9: 1
uname(BU_CMD)   9: 1
undefined behavior   1: 6, 3: 3, 12, 17–19, 21, 46, 48, 5: 3–4, 9: 17
  see also BCS conformance   3: 3
  see also unspecified property   3: 3
uninitialized data   5: 3
union   3: 5
  function argument   3: 25
  return value   3: 21
<unistd.h>   6: 83
unsigned   3: 4, 8
unspecified behavior   1: 6
unspecified property   3: 3, 18, 21, 45–47, 4: 2–3, 5–8, 12–14, 17–20, 5: 2
  see also BCS conformance   3: 3
  see also undefined behavior   3: 3

V

<varargs.h> 3: 58
variable argument list 3: 24, 58
variables, automatic 3: 57
virtual addressing 3: 27, 4: 8
  bounds 3: 29
void functions 3: 19

W

<wait.h> 6: 84
word 3: 4, 16

X

X11R4 1: 2, 6: 10
xchg instruction 3: 11

Z

zero
  null pointer 3: 5
  uninitialized data 5: 3